The Way of Youth

The Way of Youth

Buddhist Common Sense for Handling Life's Questions

Daisaku Ikeda

MIDDLEWAY
PRESS

Published by Middleway Press
A division of the SGI-USA
606 Wilshire Blvd., Santa Monica, CA 90401

© 2000 Soka Gakkai

ISBN 0-9674697-0-8

Cover and Interior Design by Lightbourne

10 9 8 7 6 5

Library of Congress Cataloging-in-Publication Data

Ikeda, Daisaku.
    The way of youth : Buddhist common sense for handling life's
questions / Daisaku Ikeda.
      p. cm.
ISBN 0-9674697-0-8 (pbk. : alk. paper)
      1. Religious life--Sōka Gakkai. 2. Youth--Religious life.
3. Youth--Conduct of life. I. Title.
BQ8436 .I36 2000   00-008506
294.3'444'0835--dc21   CIP

FOREWORD

At the age of nineteen, profoundly dissatisfied with my inability to steer the course of my life and less than impressed with the direction the modern world seemed to be taking, I began practicing Buddhism. It seemed to be the only philosophy that, while never contradicting my rational, scientific view of the universe, acknowledged its mystery and wonder. Buddhism imbued the universe and our human place in it with great dignity and freedom.

In the ten years since, my appreciation for Buddhist ideas has only deepened. Perhaps more important, my personal Buddhist practice has galvanized my life in ways I never could have imagined. In so many ways, I owe these feelings of appreciation to Daisaku Ikeda. As the leader of the Soka Gakkai International, the lay Buddhist organization of which I am a member, he has worked tirelessly to encourage, and enlighten, millions of people around the world.

My fellow lay Buddhists and I chant Nam-myoho-renge-kyo each morning and evening as part of our daily practice. While I would strongly encourage absolutely anyone to try this practice for their own growth and benefit, Buddhist philosophy, particularly as it is expounded by Daisaku Ikeda, comprises a world of ideas that can be enormously beneficial to Buddhists and non-Buddhists alike. In other words, just because you don't practice Buddhism, it doesn't mean you won't get a lot out of this book. That is because, on a practical level, Buddhism is reason; it is no different from common sense.

Of course, most of us know that we don't always use our common sense, that we don't always see things reasonably. The computer science visionary Marvin Minsky has a good explanation for this. He says, "Common sense is not a simple thing. Instead, it is an immense society of hard-earned practical ideas — of multitudes of life-learned rules and exceptions, dispositions and tendencies, balances and checks." That happens also to be a fairly good description of Buddhism.

In the following pages, you will read a series of young people's questions and concerns presented to Daisaku Ikeda. Though some of the issues raised may seem simple, there are very profound ideas embedded within Mr. Ikeda's straightforward replies. His advice to us is compassionate, empowering. Through following it, we come to recognize our ability to take control of our individual destiny. On a personal note, I find he offers poignant advice concerning love and relationships that would have saved me a lot of grief had I seen it ten years ago.

Fortunately, the advice I did take strengthened my resolve to change the things about myself that were holding me back from accomplishing my creative goals. Before I started practicing Buddhism and reading Daisaku Ikeda's guidance, I couldn't bear to sing in public — I didn't like the sound of my own voice and was painfully self-conscious on stage. It is no coincidence that seven years later, my first album went gold, I was nominated for a Grammy for Best Male Vocal performance, and I toured all over the world, performing in front of millions of people.

Lately, I have been reading a lot about computers and their evolving place in our world. Suffice to say that, from all reports, the coming decades will be filled with changes we can't even imagine — changes that will completely alter the landscape of our society socially, culturally and politically. Of course, life itself is based on constant change. As many have pointed out, the only constant is change. This is why it is imperative to find a philosophy that can carry us through these times, to embrace the positive changes and show us how to deal with the negative ones.

The truly important point Mr. Ikeda constantly underlines is that it is up to us, the generation of youth, to guide these changes and to create this new world. Not only do we all have the inherent ability to affect these changes, but we have the responsibility to do so in a wise, compassionate manner.

Thanks to Daisaku Ikeda, I have found that a life led with a Buddhist perspective can be rich, fascinating and ultimately joyful. And I think that's what it's all about, being happy, creative and filled with appreciation for life in all its excellent manifestations.

— Duncan Sheik

PREFACE

"I have a dream!" were the words of Dr. Martin Luther King Jr. What are your dreams? What are your hopes? Nothing is stronger than a life full of hope.

Every day I get letters from young people all over the world, and I talk with young men and women whenever I have a chance. I find many young people who are brimming with hope and enthusiasm, but others I come across seem to be weighed down with troubles of one kind or another. Youth is a time for growth and change, but it can also be a time of great worries. Young people at times feel ill at ease in society, as though they were abandoned alone in some sort of wilderness or battlefield. They may feel there's no one they can trust, that no one cares about them, that they haven't any goal in life.

But wait! Is it right to underrate yourself so? Should you have such a low opinion of your abilities? There's no one who doesn't have some mission, some purpose in this world. And this sense of mission and purpose is what gives clear meaning and satisfaction to people's lives.

When I was nineteen, I met Josei Toda, the man who became my lifelong teacher. Even now I can never forget the kind words he spoke to me more than forty years ago, when I was going through a very difficult period. "Daisaku," he said, "young people have to have their troubles. Troubles are what make a first-rate person of you!"

Every morning, even on Sundays, Mr. Toda acted as my private tutor, instructing me in all sorts of subjects. And I have tried in the same way to talk with young people whenever I've had the chance. Out of those discussions has come the material in the book that follows. Most of these discussions of course were with young people of Japan. But the subjects we discussed — family, friends, dreams, goals in life — I am certain are of concern to young people everywhere in the world.

I and the young people I talked with in most cases had in common our practice of Nichiren Buddhism. Nichiren, a thirteenth-century Japanese Buddhist teacher and reformer, taught that each human life has infinite potential, and revealed an easily accessible way by which everyone can nurture this potential and find true happiness in life, a way that he learned from the Lotus Sutra.

This philosophy taught by Nichiren is based upon absolute respect for life and for the worth of each individual. And because I hope to share this universally valid philosophy with ordinary readers in America and other English-speaking countries, I have asked the editors of Middleway Press to help me put together this book in English, based on a series of talks I had with high school students.

Naturally, some of the questions raised in these discussions proved very difficult because I am not a specialist in the areas they touched on. I wish I could talk to each young person individually and learn exactly what is troubling that person; then perhaps I could offer a more thorough answer to each question. But I hope that my thoughts on the various issues raised will help to give readers a new perspective on the problem, a new way of thinking about it. And where problems of a special nature are involved, I urge young people to seek the advice of some older person they can trust.

Geniuses and people of spectacular talent are a small minority; the vast majority of society is made up of plain, ordinary people. I am an ordinary man with no special background. In youth I faced the same problems that most young people do — though, since I was living in Japan in the period immediately after World War II, I grew up in war-torn surroundings. This book was written with the hope that young people can perhaps benefit from the advice of someone like me, who has had a bit more experience than they have. Instead of sermons delivered by persons who claim to have some superior understanding, I hope readers will accept what I have written as advice from someone who has walked a little farther along the road of life.

I have made it one of my aims in life to help young people to have hope and confidence in their future. I myself have infinite trust in young people, and so I say to them: You are the hope of humanity! Each of you has a bright future ahead. Each of you has a precious potential waiting to be developed. Your success, your victory will be a victory for all of us. Your victory will lead the way in this century, the century of peace and humanity, the most important century for all humankind. To you go my sincerest wishes for good health, steady advancement and success in all your endeavors.

— Daisaku Ikeda

EDITOR'S NOTE

About Nam-myoho-renge-kyo

In several of his answers in *The Way of Youth*, Mr. Ikeda refers to chanting Nam-myoho-renge-kyo. This basic component of Nichiren Buddhist practice is done in at least two sessions each day — morning and evening — along with a recitation of portions of the Lotus Sutra. According to Nichiren Buddhists, Nam-myoho-renge-kyo is the Mystic Law of life and the universe and by chanting it you reveal the law in your own life, putting yourself in harmony or rhythm with the universe. At the same time you develop a robust life force and positive outlook. The word *law* here is not used in the legal sense but in the scientific sense, like the law of gravity.

To briefly explain its component parts:

Nam (devotion) — To fuse one's life with the universal Mystic Law, drawing from it infinite energy for compassionate action.

Myoho (Mystic Law) — The fundamental principle of the universe and its phenomenal manifestations.

Renge (lotus flower) — The lotus blooms and seeds at the same time, symbolizing the simultaneity of cause and effect. The lotus, which grows in a muddy swamp, also symbolizes the emergence of Buddhahood in the life of the ordinary person.

Kyo (sutra, teaching of a Buddha) — More broadly, it indicates all phenomena or the activities of all living beings.

Pronunciation Key:
Nam – Rhymes with "Tom."
Myo – Take the first syllable of *yo-yo* and add an "m."
Ho – Like in Santa Claus's "ho, ho, ho."

Ren – Like the bird "wren."
Ge – Like the word *get* without the "t."
Kyo – Take the first syllable of *yo-yo* and add a "k."

For more information on Nichiren Buddhism and its practical applications in daily life, consult *The Buddha In Your Mirror*, available from Middleway Press in Summer 2000.

CONTENTS

FAMILY

1

- Nagging Parents

- Expressing Individuality

- Too Little Money

- Getting Along With Parents

- Handling Advice

- Too Many Restrictions

NAGGING PARENTS

My parents are always nagging me. I can't stand to be home for more than ten minutes!

How often have I heard that! While, of course, there are those who have good, open family communication, many young people get angry at their parents for telling them what to do. Often they end up not speaking to them at all.

I, too, fought with my mother from time to time about how I chose to live my life. I'd say: "Leave me alone! Let me do things my way!"

Mothers and fathers always seem to be giving their kids a hard time. From prehistoric times, mothers have been saying things like: "Do your homework!" "Turn off the television!" "Wake up or you'll be late!" It's not something we can change. But you'll understand how your parents feel when you become a parent yourself.

So it is important for you to be big-hearted. If a parent yells at you, you can think: "A loud voice means she is healthy; that's great," or, "Oh, he is expressing his love for me. I appreciate it." Your ability to view parents in this way is a sign of your increasing maturity.

Throughout the animal world, parents teach their young how to survive — how to hunt, how to eat, etc. Accordingly, our parents teach us so many things, launching us in the right direction. This is something we learn to appreciate as we become adults ourselves.

There is a well-known story about a forlorn young man sitting dejectedly by the road after quarreling with his father. He believed his father was narrow-minded, unfair and a fool. An older acquaintance came along and, guessing the cause of his sadness, said: "When I was around eighteen, my father told me nothing but dull, stupid things that infuriated me. I got really sick of hearing them. But ten years later, I started feeling that everything my father was saying made a lot of sense. I wondered, 'When did my father develop so much wisdom?'"

I think it's important that you use your own wisdom to avoid fighting with your parents. Furthermore, when your parents quarrel between themselves, as many do from time to time, the wisest thing is for you to stay out of it.

EXPRESSING INDIVIDUALITY

My parents are always criticizing my clothes and my hair. But these express who I am.

I can well imagine that you feel your individuality is being restricted if you are forced to do what your parents tell you. Expressing your individuality, however, and simply rebelling for rebellion's sake are two different things altogether.

As part of a larger whole — be it a family or social group — it's important for us to have the spirit and wisdom to get along with others. Being flexible and accommodating different views are signs of a solid sense of self. Rather than blindly following the crowd or blindly rebelling against it, it's crucial that we seek balance and harmony. To demonstrate such wisdom shows a strong self-identity.

It's a huge mistake to allow ourselves to become self-absorbed and insensitive to those around us. No one is an island. We live surrounded by our family, our friends and the rest of the world. We are all connected. The key is to display our individuality while living harmoniously within that web of relationships.

True individuality is not self-centered. It is a way of life that leads both ourselves and others in a positive direction in the most natural of ways.

TOO LITTLE MONEY

Everything I want to do takes money — and I don't have any! I wish my family was rich.

You may come from a poor family and feel frustrated because you can't buy the things you want. Maybe your parents struggle just to pay the rent much less provide extras for you. These are not uncommon situations. Many young people are in the same boat as you. Often they think that money equals happiness. But they are making a grave mistake.

Being born in a stately mansion is no guarantee of happiness, any more than being born in a shack dooms one to misery. Whether a person is happy or unhappy has nothing to do with how many material possessions he or she has. Even an affluent and seemingly enviable family can be struggling with some serious problem that may not be apparent. Often people may appear happy, but underneath they may be hiding some personal agony. No matter how together people might appear on the outside, it's difficult to see what's inside their hearts. So never be ashamed over your economic status. What's disgraceful is to have an impoverished heart, to live dishonestly.

A world-renowned businessman once told me: "Even though I have achieved fame and fortune, I felt a greater sense of purpose and fulfillment when I was poor. I had goals, and life was filled with challenge. To regain that sense of fulfillment, I realize now that I have to create a new goal: to contribute to the well-being and happiness of others."

We often see people embroiled in bitter battles over money; people plunged into misery and depression if their popularity should fade; people ruining their lives when they let fame and power go to their heads; and people living in luxurious homes where family members can't stand one another. Too often those who live in seemingly ideal, well-to-do, distinguished families are bound by formality, tradition and appearances. They have difficulty expressing genuine warmth, emotion and spontaneity. And too often privileged young people have difficulty setting goals and achieving them since their every need is taken care of. So when you get right down to it, do wealth, fame or luxury assure happiness? The answer is an emphatic "No."

Everything depends on your viewpoint. Instead of thinking you're unfortunate just because your parents don't have a lot of money or lack education, adopt the view that this is a common situation. You will see that this perspective will allow you to develop into a truly humane person. You'll realize that your hardships are the very material that will enable you to develop a big heart and become an individual of depth and substance.

The fact is, it's only by experiencing difficulties that you can become the kind of person who can understand others' feelings. Your pain and sorrow will cultivate the earth of your inner being. And from there, you can bring forth the beautiful flower of compassion and a desire to work for people's happiness.

Money, fame and material possessions offer only fleeting satisfaction, something that can be called "relative" happiness. Buddhist practitioners learn, however, to establish absolute happiness by transforming their lives from within. When we develop a state of mind as vast and resplendent as a magnificent palace, then nothing — no matter where we go or what we may encounter in life — can undermine or destroy our happiness.

GETTING ALONG
WITH PARENTS

I wish I had better parents.

E very family has its own set of circumstances and problems that only its members can fully understand. You
may wonder why you were born into your family. Or why
your parents aren't as kind as others. Or why you are not
blessed with a more beautiful home and a more loving and
supportive family. You may even want to leave home. One
thing I can say, however, is that no matter what kind of
people your parents are, they are *your* parents. If you did not
have them, you would not be alive. Please understand the
deep significance of this point. You were born to this particular family in this particular place and on this planet Earth at
this particular time. You were not born into any other family.
This fact encompasses the meaning of everything.

Buddhism explains that nothing happens by chance and
that people already possess within them all that they need
to be happy. Therefore, there is no treasure more precious
than life itself. No matter how difficult your situation, no
matter how much you feel ignored by your parents, you are
alive now — still young and blessed with a youthful spirit
with which you can construct the happiest of lives from this
moment forward. Do not destroy or harm your precious
future by giving way to despair today.

Courageously spur yourself on, reminding yourself that
the deeper the pain and grief, the greater the happiness that
awaits you. Have the determination to become a pillar of
support for your family. Buddhism teaches this way of life.
Whether you have a parent suffering from alcoholism or a

serious illness, whether your family is experiencing difficult times because of a parent's failed business, whether you have to endure the pain of seeing a parent criticized and attacked even falsely, or whether you are abandoned by a parent — all of these seemingly adverse situations can be viewed as nourishment to make you grow even stronger.

Regardless of how you are treated by your parents, ultimately, it is your responsibility, not theirs, that you become happy. It is up to each of us to have the determination to become the "sun" that can dispel all the darkness in our lives and within our families. Nichiren Buddhists know that this resolve can be fortified by chanting Nam-myoho-renge-kyo each morning and evening.

No matter what happens, it is vital that you live confidently with the conviction that you are the "sun." Of course, in life there are sunny days and cloudy days. But even on cloudy days, the sun is still shining. Even if we are suffering, it is vital that we strive to keep the sun shining brightly in our hearts.

One young person I know has no father, his mother is incapacitated by serious health problems, and his older sister is in the hospital. While enduring so many hardships in youth, he has already scaled a high mountain in life, well ahead of others. I believe that young people who confront such hardships will be the leaders of the twenty-first century.

HANDLING ADVICE

I don't like it when people, especially my parents, point out my shortcomings.

One of the more frustrating things in life is when we think we are one way, while the people around us think we are just the opposite. Other people, however, can often see things about us that we can't. This is good, because in the same way that a mirror allows you to see your face, the people around you can serve as a mirror to let you see many other aspects of yourself.

The comments of people close to you can help you focus your individuality in a positive direction. The education, guidance, advice, warnings and even rebukes you receive can all be used constructively to steer you along the right path. On the other hand, refusing to listen to others' advice, rebelliously doing only what you want and making things unpleasant for everyone under the guise of expressing your individuality are just forms of stubbornness that don't benefit anyone.

Having people point out your shortcomings and help you weed out your bad habits at the root allows you, in the long run, to forge your individuality in a way that will be of value to you. If, on the other hand, the roots of those bad habits remain, they will gradually affect your life adversely, moving you in a harmful, destructive direction. When you can realize this, you will see that refusing to listen to advice is foolish. It's important to be wise.

TOO MANY RESTRICTIONS

My parents place too many restrictions on me. They don't seem to understand that I'm not a kid anymore. How can I convince them of this?

I can certainly understand what you're saying. No one likes to be controlled by others, and it's only natural to wish we could do our own thing without people hassling us all the time. I know some students dream of the freedom they would enjoy if there were no rules, if they had plenty of money and time and no parents nagging them. But, really, that is a superficial perspective of human society.

Real freedom ultimately hinges on what you decide to dedicate yourself to with all your heart. It doesn't mean loafing around with nothing to do. It isn't spending money like water. It isn't having all the free time in the world. It isn't taking long vacations. Doing only as you please is not freedom — it is nothing more than self-indulgence. True freedom lies in the ongoing challenge to develop yourself, to achieve your chosen goal.

F R I E N D S H I P 2

- Genuine Friendship

- Choosing Good Friends

- Good Friends vs. Bad Friends

- Losing Friends

- Handling Rejection

- Peer Pressure

- Keeping Friends

- People You Don't Like

- Dealing With Envy

- Being a Loner

- Advising Friends

GENUINE FRIENDSHIP

How can I tell who my real friends are?

First, it is a good idea to consider what friendship is. True friendship is a relationship where you empathize with your friends when they are suffering and encourage them not to lose heart. And they, in turn, do the same for you.

Friendship often begins simply by liking someone because he or she spends a lot of time with you or, perhaps, helps you with your homework. You may start by liking someone who is nice to you and with whom you get along well and have a lot in common. While friendships may begin spontaneously and develop by themselves, deep friendships are supported by a spirit to grow and advance. Between you and your friends there must be a commitment to always be there to encourage and help one another as you work toward your respective goals in life.

To have some ambition, such as graduating from a university or making a meaningful contribution to society, is important. Those who lack a clear, positive purpose or direction in life tend to have friendships that lead nowhere or are based on dependency. In some cases, these types of friendships actually encourage destructive behavior. But friendships among people who cheerfully encourage one another while striving to realize their dreams are the kind that deepen and endure.

Character and integrity are indispensable for making friends. True friendship is unconcerned with social status or rank. You can make real friends only when you open up, when you share with others what's in your heart. A selfish, egotistical person cannot make true friends.

The tie that links one person's heart to another is sincerity. For adults, self-interest or personal gain often comes into play, and fleeting friendships are formed as the result of temporary circumstance. But friendships made in one's youth are generally free of artificiality. Nothing is more wonderful or precious than the true friendships formed when you are young.

Your friends from junior high and high school, even elementary school, are like your fellow actors, appearing in the same play with you on the stage of life. Some you may never forget for the rest of your life.

Such friendships flow as beautifully as a pure, fresh stream. The clear and unspoiled currents of two people converge in sincerity, moving positively toward their respective dreams. Struggling and growing together, they share each other's hardships, always encouraging and supporting each other, creating an even broader, deeper and purer river of friendship. The beauty and clarity of this river will inspire all who see it to want to drink from its waters, too.

Friendship is true wealth. There have been many famous sayings about it throughout the ages, such as Cicero's "Friendship is closer than kinship" and "A life without friendship is like a world without sunshine" and Aristotle's "A friend is like another self." No matter how much status or wealth people may gain, those without friends are indeed sad and lonely. A life without friendship leads to an unbalanced, self-centered existence.

CHOOSING GOOD FRIENDS

I want to have good friends in my life. What do you suggest?

You are wise to understand the importance of friendship. You probably have many different kinds of friends — friends who live in the same neighborhood and with whom you go to school every day; friends in the same class; friends in extracurricular activities; friends with whom you just hang out. Sometimes, too, friendship starts out as a casual thing, with two people just sitting around talking. Then one day something happens that inspires them both to try to achieve some goal. They then become good friends who positively influence each other. The best friends to have are those with whom you can advance together toward a shared goal. While we can't choose our family, we can choose our friends. And it's an important choice. I often hear, "School is fun because I have friends there." Others lament, "I have friends, but I don't have any close enough to speak with heart to heart."

You were born into this vast universe on the tiny planet Earth and in the same era as the people around you. Yet it is extremely rare to find, among the billions of people on this planet, genuine, unconditional friends with whom you can totally be yourself, who will understand your thoughts and feelings even without words.

Among your fellow students, I'm sure most of you have at least one or two whom you regard as true friends — please treasure them. But if you feel that you don't have any close friends right now, don't worry. Just tell yourself that you will have wonderful friends in the future. Concentrate your energies now on becoming a fine individual who is considerate, who does not speak badly of others, and who does not go back on your word. I'm sure that in the future you will have many friends, perhaps all over the world.

In any event, it's important to understand that friendship depends on you, not on the other person. It all comes down to your attitude, what you are willing to contribute to the relationship. I hope you will not be a fair-weather friend, helping others only when circumstances are good and leaving them high and dry when problems occur; instead, strive to become a person who sticks by friends no matter what.

You can prepare your life for great friendships by what you do today. There are things you can do to become the kind of great friend you hope to have. For example, when you notice someone is worried about something, offer a kind word: "You look down. What's wrong?" Treat others' problems as your own and try to help. This kind of strong resolve is important.

And if someone should betray your trust, vow to yourself that you'll never do the same thing to anyone else. When you make a promise, always keep it, no matter what. If you make an effort to be that kind of person, you'll soon come to find yourself surrounded by good friends.

GOOD FRIENDS
VS. BAD FRIENDS

My parents don't approve of the friends I hang out with.

Parents who worry about the friends you keep are truly concerned about your welfare. The same can be said of teachers. They're not just trying to give you a hard time.

Your friends, at times, can have a stronger influence over you than your parents or anyone else. So if you make good friends — friends who are interested in improving and developing themselves — you can move in a positive direction as well. Associating with self-destructive people, however, can have harmful consequences, dragging you down with them. Please have the courage not to give in to negative influences and to move away from those who cause you to behave in a way in which you are not comfortable.

Buddhism teaches that we should associate with good companions, meaning that we should be careful to choose good people as our friends and role models. It also instructs that we should distance ourselves from bad company. A relationship based on selfish motives or spoiled by hassles over money cannot be considered a good friendship. Similarly, a relationship with someone who engages in delinquent behavior, who doesn't know right from wrong, is clearly a bad friendship. A real friend will not demand money from you or encourage you to do things that are wrong. That is evil disguised as friendship. You must speak out against it and avoid getting involved. Don't prolong an association with bad friends. It's perfectly all right to walk away from such company. Discuss your situation with someone you trust. Don't just worry silently over it by yourself.

A Buddhist scripture states that even a good person who associates with evil people will likely be tainted by that evil, therefore we should be strict with ourselves about pointing out wrong and destructive behavior. And by pointing out to others that their actions are inflicting suffering and pain, we can urge them to move in a more positive direction. In fact, our honesty can open the way to forging deep bonds of genuine friendship with that person. In other words, it's quite possible for a "bad" friend to become a good friend.

Bad companions are those who cause people trouble and grief. Good friends, in contrast, are those who warmly encourage others, giving them hope and inspiring them to self-improvement. True friendship contributes to our growth as people and the creation of positive value in our lives. We cannot say the same of associating with bad influences, where the only result is stagnation and negativity — that is just hanging out together, not friendship. As a well-known saying goes, "You can judge a person by the company he (or she) keeps."

Ultimately, the only way to make good friends is for you to become a good friend yourself by maintaining your integrity. Good people gather around other good people.

LOSING FRIENDS

What do you do when a friend suddenly doesn't want to talk to you anymore?

Young people's hearts are like sensitive thermometers. One minute you feel everything is great, and the next you suddenly feel so down you're convinced you must be the most worthless person in the world. You may also be overwhelmed by great sadness and despair because of problems with friends, heartache over love or the illness of family members.

I assure you it is completely natural to experience such extremes of emotion and self-doubt while young, so you needn't compound your sadness by worrying that you feel that way. Rest assured that whatever your hardships, you will someday look back on them and they will all seem like a dream.

That said, it is important to recognize that as you go through such situations, the same is usually true for your friends. Therefore, the best thing to do is to have the courage to ask the friend who seems to be shunning you what's bothering her (or him). You will very likely find that the last thing she wanted to do was treat you coldly, and that in reality, while you neglected to find out what was wrong with her for fear of being hurt, she, too, was feeling rejected and lonely.

Human relationships are like a mirror. If you're thinking, "If only so-and-so were a little nicer to me, I could talk to him about how I feel," that person is probably thinking the same thing.

While it takes a bit of courage to make the initial

attempt, a good plan would be to make the first move to open channels of communication. If, despite these efforts, you are still rebuffed, then the person you should feel sorry for is your friend.

We cannot read what's in another's heart; the human heart is much too complex. People change—it's as simple as that. If your friend shares the same feelings about the friendship as you do, then it is likely to last a long time. But if he or she decides to opt out, then it will be short-lived. You yourself may unintentionally let a friend down, causing a rift in your relationship. My advice is that you hold fast to your identity regardless of how others may appear to change.

If you *are* snubbed or let down by others, have the strength of character to vow that you will never do the same to anyone else. Though they usually do not realize it, those who betray others' trust are only hurting themselves. Those who intentionally hurt their friends are truly pathetic; it's as though they are driving a spike through their own hearts.

Character and integrity are very important. Mutual respect and trust are crucial for creating real friendship. Naturally, there will be times when you have arguments and disagreements with your friends. But there should always be an underlying spirit of respect and consideration for each other. In friendship, we mustn't think only of ourselves.

In any event, should a friendship end, there's no need to grow despondent. You don't have to beat yourself up, thinking every friendship must last forever. The important thing is that you remember the true meaning of friendship and that you make that true meaning the basis for your interactions with others.

If one friend lets you down, don't stop trusting people;

go and make a new friend. If you don't trust anyone, you might avoid being hurt or let down, but you'll find yourself leading a lonely existence locked up in your shell. The fact is, only someone who has experienced pain and hardship can empathize with others and treat them with kindness. The essential thing to do, therefore, is to become strong.

F
R
I
E
N
D
S
H
I
P

HANDLING REJECTION

What about when a whole group of friends gives you the cold shoulder?

Allow me to share the following story of a young woman, a high school student, who practices Nichiren Buddhism. At school, Mikki was part of a close-knit group of seven. As the girls spent more and more time together, they became increasingly aware of one another's strengths and shortcomings and gradually began to gossip about any member who wasn't present. Mikki did not take part in these gossip sessions and tried to persuade them to stop. But the other six used her refusal to participate as an excuse to turn on her.

In class, they gave Mikki cold looks. They handed her nasty notes. If they happened to touch her accidentally, they would scream as if in horror and run away. Each day was agony. With each indignity inflicted on her, Mikki felt as if her heart was being torn out. In her free time, she'd hide in the girls' bathroom to avoid further humiliation.

Finding no peer she could trust, Mikki finally confided to her mother about her problems at school. Her mother encouraged her to use this trying period to develop her own inner foundation through her faith. Mikki realized that as she chanted Nam-myoho-renge-kyo, she began to feel stronger and happier. And though she still frequently experienced torment at school, it was affecting her less. She began to view her suffering as fuel, as the perfect motivation to become solid and happy within herself.

Mikki continued to chant each day with the feeling, "I won't be defeated! I will become strong!" Going to school became steadily less of a problem. Based on her newfound strength, she decided to take positive action to change her situation. She made new friends and, in the end, she even changed her relationship with the members of the original group that had shunned her. Mikki says that she actually feels grateful to them, because they inspired her to become stronger and more independent. The secret, she says, to getting others to change is to become a stronger person yourself.

F
R
I
E
N
D
S
H
I
P

HANDLING REJECTION

Sometimes when I try to make new friends, it's like I'm not cool enough for them, and I'm left on the outside looking in.

Although it may seem difficult, if you are ignored, rejected or made fun of, try not to be overly worried about it. According to Buddhist beliefs, those who treat others poorly make bad causes for which they unfortunately will experience the effects; they are truly to be pitied.

At the same time, remember that experiencing rejection and disappointment is an inevitable part of life. Nichiren, whose teachings we in the Soka Gakkai International follow, was also abandoned by many of his followers. I, too, have been betrayed by people whom I trusted and sincerely tried to encourage. But that is something I have learned is inevitable at times.

In the face of rejection, you must learn to be courageous. It is important to believe in yourself. Be like the sun, which shines on serenely even though not all the heavenly bodies reflect back its light and even though some of its brilliance seems to radiate only into empty space. While those who reject your friendship may sometimes fade out of your life, the more you shine your light, the more brilliant your life will become.

No matter what other people do, it is important that you walk your own path, believing in yourself. If you stay true to yourself, others will definitely come to understand your sincere intent.

PEER PRESSURE

There's a lot of peer pressure among my school friends to drink and smoke marijuana.

I can understand the feelings of young people when they sometimes want to take drugs or drink to be part of the group. But drinking alcohol or taking drugs in your teens is not an adventure that will contribute constructively to your life. And having free access to these things doesn't foster your freedom as a human being, as so many young people believe. If your friends drink and take drugs, look for a new group of friends.

Drinking or taking drugs is actually a trap, and once you are ensnared in that trap, your true independence is stripped from you. You become bound by your emotions and your cravings for more of those substances. Those who become victims of their own natures and cravings are, strictly speaking, no different from beasts.

In 1275, referring to a teaching from thousands of years earlier, Nichiren offered this timeless advice to a follower: "Become the master of your mind rather than letting your mind master you."

Essentially, substance abuse can be pegged to one underlying condition — a lack of foresight and determination toward the future. So many youth have been robbed of the chance to fulfill their great potential because they did not maintain a focus on their goals. Pursuing fun in the moment led them to ruin. I believe you may be familiar with many famous examples, such as the superstar college basketball player who was drafted by the Boston Celtics. Expectations of him were so high, it seemed his presence would guarantee a championship team. Sadly, just before the beginning of his first season — before he even got a chance to play in his first pro game — he went to a party, overdosed on cocaine and died. A tragic waste.

In so many ways, what separates those who go on to lead happy, fulfilling and successful lives from those who do not are the choices they make during this crucial period. Those who choose to keep their dreams in sight weigh the importance of achieving those dreams against the momentary "coolness" of surrendering to drinking and drugs and find such immediate gratification not worth the expense.

Some people may believe that drugs enhance their concentration. But I have to say that no matter how brilliant it may seem, anything drug-induced is not the product of your true ability.

The most attractive person is one who can continue to make steady efforts to fulfill his or her dream even if others do not recognize their dedication. A person of self-control is a truly cool person. Continuing to challenge your goals is vital.

While it is socially acceptable for those of legal drinking age to enjoy alcohol in moderation, it is important to understand that the trap of addiction does not simply go away when you reach twenty-one. If that were the case, obviously, alcoholism would not be such a global tragedy among adults. Again, I cannot stress too strongly the need to establish your dreams in your youth and hold them firmly in sight. They will be the best gauge for measuring all your actions.

KEEPING FRIENDS

I enjoy the friends I have. How can I keep them as time goes on?

While we would prefer our friendships to continue, our focus is better spent, I believe, on developing the quality of those relationships. Toward that end we can classify friendships into three groups according to their depth.

The first level is composed of people who get along with one another in the course of their day-to-day activities and seek to enjoy their lives together. These are friendships based on having a good time together.

The second level of friendship is a little more advanced. These friends have their own goals; they each have a clear vision of the kind of person they want to become, the kind of future they want to build, the kind of contribution they wish to make to humanity. They encourage and support one another as they each work to realize their own dreams and make something of themselves in the world. This is a friendship of mutual encouragement.

I have heard from many high school students about that kind of friendship: "We worked together and built an incredible display for the science fair," "Before every test, we study together," "As members of the swim team, we all challenged ourselves to swim six miles, and all of us did it! It's something I'm never going to forget."

Many, many students have recognized that they are not alone, and knowing that has given them the strength to overcome tough challenges. They have come to appreciate mutual encouragement and support.

The third level of friendship is the bond of comrades

who share the same ideals, who dedicate their lives to a common cause. Many people who have achieved great things in history have had this kind of friendship, which demands absolute trust. True comrades never betray one another, not even under the threat of death. They never betray themselves, their friends or their ideals.

I hope you enjoy the time you spend with your peers without worrying about how long your friendship will last. Deep friendships are rare. Cultivating them is like growing a mighty tree — a different process than that for growing shrubs.

If you remain sincere in your interactions with others, you will one day find yourself surrounded by good friends. And among those people, your friendships will be as strong and unshakable as towering trees. *Don't be impatient.* Work first on developing yourself, and you can rest assured that an infinite number of wonderful encounters await you in the future.

PEOPLE YOU DON'T LIKE

What do I do about the people I just can't get along with?

J ust as there are some foods you find distasteful, having people in your environment whom you dislike is an unavoidable part of life. While there's nothing wrong with not particularly liking certain people, it is wrong to put them down or behave in a hostile way toward them. They have the same right to exist as you do and to have their own opinions and ways of doing things. It's important to culti-vate a broad-minded outlook. Also, Buddhism teaches the interrelatedness of all people and things, and how we treat others will affect our own lives — so it is important to be respectful in our behavior both for others' sake as well as for our own.

DEALING WITH ENVY

I strive to get good grades, but often my friends make me feel bad about my achievements.

Always be proud of your hard work! Outstanding people are bound to encounter envy and resentment, so don't worry — that's life. A philosopher once said: "We live in a world where even if one has impeccable character, he or she will inevitably be slandered and criticized." Of course, I am not suggesting that you go around boasting to everyone about your good grades, either.

When I was in elementary school, one student from an affluent family was always well dressed and seemed so happy. I remember feeling jealous of him, and I wasn't alone. Today, out of such jealously, that student would almost certainly be picked on by his classmates. But those who take action based on such feelings are driven by a base condition of life, what Buddhism terms animality. The brilliance of true humanity, on the other hand, lies in surmounting feelings of envy with the resolute attitude, "I'll create an even more wonderful life for myself." If you are jealous of others, you will not advance; you will only become miserable. Rather than being so easily defeated by your emotions, I hope you can embrace others with warmth and understanding.

BEING A LONER

What if I like being by myself more than being in a group?

Of course, you're free to enjoy your own company if you wish. It's perfectly all right to make friends in your own way, with people whose thoughts and feelings you share.

Sometimes our relations with others can get so difficult that we want to shout, "I wish I could live where there are no other people!" But unless we become hermits, that's impossible. It's important that we work to become individuals who can cultivate good relations with others.

In Japanese, we write the word for "human being" with the characters meaning "person" and "between," expressing the idea that human beings are complete only in relationship to other people. None of us can live alone. Because of that, experiencing relationship problems of some sort is an inevitable part of human life.

Relationship problems are opportunities to grow and mature. Such problems can be character building if you don't let them defeat you. That's why it's important not to isolate yourself. No one can exist apart from others. Remaining aloof from others cultivates selfishness, which accomplishes nothing.

Having close friends can be tremendously rewarding. There's a Mongolian proverb, "A hundred friends are more precious than a hundred pieces of gold." People who have friends are rich. Quite often, the encouragement and stimulation of friends spur us toward self-improvement. We are inspired to lead fulfilling lives and create a better world. We also work together with our friends toward that goal.

Having good friends is like being equipped with a powerful auxiliary engine. When we encounter a steep hill or an obstacle, we can encourage one another and find the strength to keep pressing forward vigorously.

ADVISING FRIENDS

I know people who do some really bad things, but when I try to talk to them about it, they don't take me seriously.

The only way you can influence your peers is to establish genuine friendships with them one by one.

Listen attentively to what they have to say, but also clearly tell them when their ideas are wrong and admonish them not to ruin their lives through their actions. Develop the type of friendship in which you can say what needs to be said.

Nichiren teaches that if we befriend someone but lack the mercy to correct that person, we are in fact his or her enemy. How you convey your message to someone moving in the wrong direction is a matter of wisdom. Through serious contemplation based on your deep desire to help your friend, and through candid discussion with someone you trust — like a teacher or parent — you can find an upsurge of courage from within. This is what's behind the Buddhist chant of Nam-myoho-renge-kyo — it allows us to tap our inner wisdom and courage so that we can become the kind of people who truly care about and positively influence our friends.

As long as you genuinely care about others, your heart will definitely reach them some day. Even if someone breaks off with you for a while because of what you have said or done, the fact that you showed your sincerity will be etched in the depths of his or her life. The seed you plant in your friend's life will one day sprout in the form of a new and positive awareness that can propel that friend forward.

L O V E 3

LOVE

TRUE LOVE

Having a crush on or dating someone makes life more exciting!

Being attracted to someone can be wonderful. When you fall in love, life seems filled with drama and excitement; you feel like the leading character in a novel. Otherwise, much of daily life tends to be ordinary and unexciting, and making steady efforts day by day can be trying. It's not always fun. The question is: Does that person inspire you to work harder or distract you? Does his or her presence make you more determined to devote greater energies to school activities, be a better friend, a more thoughtful son or daughter? Does he or she inspire you to realize your future goals and work to achieve them? Or is that person your central focus, overshadowing all else?

If you are neglecting things, forgetting your purpose in life because you have a crush, then you're on the wrong path. A healthy relationship is one in which two people encourage each other to reach their respective goals while sharing each other's hopes and dreams. A relationship should be a source of inspiration, invigoration and hope.

Dante Alighieri, one of the greatest Western medieval poets, had a young woman named Beatrice as his source of inspiration. He had loved her from afar since childhood. One day, after a long time apart, the eighteen-year-old Dante ran into her again on the street. He later composed a poem about his joy at that encounter, titled "Revitalization." In his struggle to convey his feelings for the young woman, he created a new poetic form. Beatrice had unlocked Dante's artistic potential.

She would remain, however, an unrequited love, for she married another man and died very young. But Dante never stopped loving her. Ultimately, that love enabled him to strengthen and deepen the capacity of his heart and create something truly noble and sublime. In his masterpiece, *The Divine Comedy*, Dante depicts Beatrice as a gentle, benevolent being who guides him to Heaven.

Of course, Dante lived in a different age from ours. But I think many things can be learned from this great poet who stayed true to his feelings, whether or not they were reciprocated, and transformed them into his life's inspiration. I truly believe that love must be a guiding inspiration for our lives, the driving force for us to live courageously.

If you use love as an escape, the euphoria is unlikely to last long. If anything, you may only find yourself with even more problems — along with a great deal of pain and sadness. However much we may try, we can never run away from ourselves. If we remain weak, suffering will follow us wherever we go. We will never find happiness if we don't change ourselves from within.

Let me also add that to treat a relationship simply as an escape, even if you are not consciously aware of it, is extremely disrespectful to both your partner and yourself.

Happiness is not something that someone else, like a girlfriend or boyfriend, can give us. We have to achieve it for ourselves. And the only way to do so is by developing our character and capacity as human beings, by fully realizing our own potential. If we sacrifice our growth and talent for love, we absolutely will not find happiness.

While in your teens, your scope of experience is still limited. You may not yet have found the area in which your talents are best expressed. Even if you have, it's easy to fall into the trap of thinking that nothing could be more desirable than romantic love. But there is more to life.

The point is not to be in a hurry. In fact, not being in a relationship can be beneficial. It allows you time to study and to participate in extracurricular activities, which help you build a foundation for a strong self. Being alone is not something to be afraid of, because when the time is right you will find the right someone to love. You are young. What's important now is to work hard at developing yourself into a truly wonderful human being.

You have a precious mission—something important to contribute to the betterment of others—that only you can fulfill. Suffering people around the world are waiting for your brave endeavors. To neglect your special mission and seek only personal pleasure are signs of selfishness. It is impossible for an egotistic, self-centered individual to truly love another person.

On the other hand, if you genuinely love someone, then through your relationship with him or her, you can develop into a person whose love extends to all humanity. That sort of relationship strengthens and enriches your inner realm. Ultimately, the relationships you form reflect your own state of life. Only to the extent that you polish yourself now can you hope to develop wonderful bonds of the heart in the future.

L
O
V
E

TAKE YOUR TIME

It seems like everything in our culture — from advertising to movies and TV sitcoms — tells us that sex and romance are what will make us happy.

The message carried by some of the media and other influences on youth reflects a warped adult society that exploits the minds of young people. They create programming for profit without a thought for the well-being of the youth today.

Swayed by popular images and peer pressure, many young people are in a hurry to start dating. They seem to feel they are missing out if they don't have a boyfriend or girlfriend when TV and movies tell them that everyone else around them does.

But don't get caught up in doing something just because it seems that everyone else is. It is so important that you see these things for what they are. Your youth is precious. *Each of you is valuable beyond measure.* It is foolish to become manipulated by pop culture. Instead, I hope you will resolutely follow your own path in life.

To give in to the view that being in love is the be-all and end-all of life is to delude yourself that as long as you are in love, nothing else matters. It is a misguided notion that sinking ever deeper into a painful and possibly destructive relationship is somehow cool.

Buddhism is based on common sense and reason. Accordingly, it teaches that there is a time for everything in life — a time to be young, a time to enter the adult world, a time to get married and so on. Moving forward step by step into each phase is in accord with reason.

In the Buddhist scriptures, called sutras, is a story of a wealthy man who is envious of another's beautiful, three-story home. And so he hires a carpenter to build him a mansion of equal grandeur. The carpenter agrees and naturally begins building from the foundation up, but the rich man is impatient and says: "I don't want a foundation. And I don't want a first or second floor. I just want a mansion that is three stories high. Hurry up and build the third floor!" This may seem like a silly story, but there are many people who behave this way.

Just as a house will eventually fall down if it has no foundation or if the foundation is laid carelessly, it's clear what kind of results you can expect if you take shortcuts. Similarly, it is unwise to try to live like an adult before you can properly look after yourself.

All too often, when a relationship ends, the great passion it once inspired seems an illusion. The things you learn from studying, on the other hand, are permanent. It is important, therefore, that you never let a relationship extinguish the flame of your intellectual curiosity.

The important thing is for you to do your very best at what you have to concentrate on *now*. Through such efforts, you will grow into individuals with truly wonderful futures. I hope you will not sell yourself short and stifle your limitless potential. Far too many people nip their brilliant promise in the bud in the blind pursuit of romance. As the saying "love is blind" reminds us, people can lose their objectivity when they fall in love.

L
O
V
E

STAYING TRUE TO YOURSELF

Sometimes when I'm in a relationship, it's like I'm not myself. I try hard to be what the other person wants me to be.

It is demeaning to constantly seek your partner's approval. In such relationships real caring, depth or even love is missing. If you are not being treated the way your heart says you should be, I hope you will have the courage and dignity to decide you are better off risking your partner's scorn than enduring unhappiness.

A shallow person will have only shallow relationships. Real love is not one person clinging to another; it can only be fostered between two strong people secure in their individuality. Rather than becoming so love-struck it seems only the two of you exist, it is much healthier to continue making efforts to improve and develop yourself while learning from those aspects of your partner that you respect and admire. Antoine de Saint-Exupéry, author of *The Little Prince*, wrote in a work called *Wind, Sand and Stars*, "Love is not two people gazing at each other, but two people looking ahead together in the same direction." Relationships last longer when both partners share similar values and beliefs.

True love is not about doing whatever the other person wants or pretending you are something you're not. Someone who genuinely loves you will not insist that you do anything against your will or embroil you in some dangerous activity.

Without respect, no relationship will last very long nor can two people bring out the best in each other. I personally hope men will be extremely courteous and caring toward women, respecting them and doing their utmost to support them. The responsibility of men is to become strong enough, compassionate enough and adult enough to care about the lifelong happiness of their partners. For men who strive to cultivate this quality, it is also an expression of true love.

Also, it is important to think about when you have children of your own — when they fall in love, how would you like to see them treated? If you can't imagine that scenario, you are not yet ready for love.

I think it's important for everyone to have at least one person with whom they can talk about anything — especially about love. I am in particular concerned about those who have closed themselves off from their friends and family — it's fine to keep some things to yourself, but sometimes secrets may hurt you. In matters concerning love, it is to your benefit to accept that you are not necessarily the best judge of your situation and to have the wisdom to turn to others for their objective opinions and advice.

No matter how much you may appear to be enjoying yourself now or how serious you think you are about your relationship, if you allow your love life to consume your time and energy at the expense of your growth, then you're just playing a game. And if you're always playing games, then your life will be just that, a game.

L
O
V
E

ADDICTED TO LOVE

What do you think about people who always have to be in a relationship, who can't stand ever being alone?

Every person has the freedom to live his or her own way, and each person's character is different. Nevertheless, I think it's a shame to be constantly chasing after love.

If someone is going to fall in love, wouldn't it be wonderful if that love led to marriage? And how much more wonderful would it be to have one great love that lasts a lifetime? Of course, this won't always happen. Nevertheless, it is unfair to enter into a relationship with someone if you haven't decided that you are committed to making it a serious one and instead are always on the lookout for a replacement should this one sour.

If you do have a friend who feels she must always be in a relationship, why don't you talk to her heart to heart? Try to explain that the future holds unlimited possibilities. There is no need to rush into anything; there is no need to be in a hurry to grow up. If your friend likes someone, there's nothing wrong with holding that feeling inside her heart while resolving to polish herself so that she can become the kind of person anyone would be proud to be with. Self-development is the foundation for your happy relationships in the future.

PROTECTING YOURSELF

How do you know when someone's just using you?

The fact is, some boys are only out to use girls to satisfy their sexual impulses. So girls have to be on their guard and cultivate their powers of wisdom and judgment in order to see through such people. Girls, too, can initiate sexual relationships, though usually their motivation is to deepen the relationship, which can easily backfire.

If the relationship you're in is causing your parents to worry or making you neglect your studies or engage in destructive behavior, then you and the person you're seeing are only having a negative influence on each other. Neither of you will be happy, and you may end up hurting each other.

L
O
V
E

PROTECTING YOURSELF

My parents and friends are worried because I'm dating an older man. I don't see what the big deal is.

Many young women are extremely vulnerable to the insistent advances of the opposite sex, particularly those of older men. They act as though stunned and lose their ability to make calm, rational decisions. This is precisely the reason why it's vital for young women to develop inner strength and self-respect. Since they are the ones who most often get hurt, they have every right to assert their dignity and look after their welfare. If the man in question does not respect this right, then he isn't worth being with.

Some people, however, once they have gotten into a relationship, have a hard time saying "no" for fear of losing the other person. In such cases, love is like riding in a car with no brakes. Even if you regret having gotten in and want to get out, the car won't stop. People often get involved in relationships thinking they are free and independent but at some point find they have become captive to the relationship. This is as true for boys as for girls.

You are infinitely precious. Therefore, I hope you will treat yourself with utmost respect. Rather than following a path that will cause you to suffer, please take the best road for your well-being.

The truth is, ideal love is fostered only between two sincere, mature and independent people. It is essential, therefore, that you make polishing yourself a priority and do not get carried away by romance.

SEX

My boyfriend wants to have sex with me. I love him and don't want to lose him. What should I do?

That young people are interested in many things, including sex, is a natural part of their growth as human beings. You may have lifelong regrets, however, if you are blindly carried away by your physical desires.

The urge to explore that aspect is very strong, fueled by both your body and your mind, so it is important to have the right attitude and understand that the decisions you make today, the actions you take, have consequences. Your future does not exist in some far-off place. The seed for your future happiness lies in your behavior today, your frame of mind at this very moment. Therefore, it is important to think about the best kind of relationship you can have with friends, sweethearts and anyone important to you. If you fall in love, I hope you will remember that, ultimately, the best relationship is one in which both you and your partner can continue to develop yourselves.

The tendency for teens, especially, is to be blind in love. But I have to tell you, love means more than just doing whatever your boyfriend suggests. It concerns me that too many teenagers become pregnant or contract illnesses and suffer for a long time, sometimes permanently, as a result of momentary passions.

The ideal relationship is one in which you mutually aim at a great future goal, encouraging and helping each other develop. If your boyfriend really cares about you, he will not force you to do anything you don't want to do. By saying no firmly, you can see just how genuine his sincerity is.

I hope you will take the course of action that supports the sort of future you dream of and that you are not swayed by others' notions of what is cool.

TEEN PREGNANCY

What can I say to a friend who has become pregnant? Or to one who's been lucky so far but is having sex and not being careful?

Unwanted pregnancy is a tragedy. Young people have a tendency to feel invincible — that no matter what they do, things will be all right. But, while this behavior is optimistic, in truth it is reckless. No one is free from the law of cause and effect.

For those who are sexually active but have been lucky so far, consider the following:

To have an abortion, especially while very young, can be spiritually depressing and physically risky. And if you decide to go through with an unexpected pregnancy, you will more than likely have to sacrifice your freedom to enjoy activities in which others can freely participate. Your teen years are a period to build the foundation of your future happiness. It is the age when your body and mind are still very fresh and flexible, and you can absorb many things that will be important to you for the rest of your life. It is the age when you can master some skills or devote yourself to studying, in which you can freely shape your future as you please. It would be tragic to give up such great freedom so young. You will be doing a disservice not only to yourself but to your parents and others who have been caring so much about you over the years.

For your friend who became pregnant, I believe it is vital that you maintain a *genuine* friendship with her. That doesn't mean merely sympathizing with her but providing her with the strength to stand up for herself. Your friend may be hurting or at a loss. While respecting her decisions, I hope you can continue to encourage her. Tell her that no matter how difficult her immediate circumstances, she can absolutely turn her situation into something joyful. Of course, this should not be a rationale for throwing caution to the wind. It's just that no matter where we find ourselves, we should always maintain hope.

HANDLING HEARTBREAK

I recently broke up with someone, and I am really depressed.

M any people can relate to such feelings. But you are only letting yourself down if you fall victim to unhealthy obsessions or are so blinded by love you can't see anything else. No matter what, always do your best to live courageously, to be strong-hearted. Youth is a time for advancing bravely into the future. So please don't allow yourself to veer off course or fall behind or hide in the shadows.

Youth is not a time for pessimism or self-pity. That mind-set is for losers. Instead, in the face of rejection, I hope you will cultivate a resilient spirit, that you will have the confidence to think: "It's their loss if they can't appreciate how wonderful I am!"

John D. Rockefeller, the American industrialist and philanthropist who amassed a huge fortune, was such a person. In his younger days, when he was poor, he proposed to his first love, but she turned him down. Ironically, the young woman's mother wouldn't allow her daughter to marry someone whose prospects seemed so dim, a perfect example of how difficult it is to evaluate potential! Rather than feeling depressed, it seems to have been just the thing to inspire young Rockefeller.

Please don't let a broken heart discourage you. Tell yourself that you're not so weak or fragile that such a minor thing can bring you down. You may think no one could possibly compare to the person you have lost. But how will this person compare to the next ten, the next hundred, the next thousand people you will meet? You cannot declare with certainty that there won't be another who far surpasses this person in your affections. As you grow, the way you look at people will change as well.

I'm sure quite a few among you have had your hearts broken and felt unable to go on, your self-esteem in tatters. But you must never think you are worthless. No one can substitute for you, who are more precious than all the treasures in the universe put together. No matter what your present circumstances, you are irreplaceable. Please hold on to that thought, fight to overcome all obstacles and rise out of all suffering and despair.

It is crucial that you become strong. If you are strong, even your sadness will become a source of nourishment, and the things that make you suffer will purify your life. It is precisely because we have experienced great suffering that we can grow strong and become capable adults.

I have heard it said: "If you are sad, cry — cry until your tears have washed away all the pain." It's like crossing a river of suffering. Those who have done so have a depth and a radiance unknown to those who are strangers to such experience. The thing is not to drown in the river.

What's important is to keep moving forward. If you use your sadness as a source of growth, you will become a person of greater depth and breadth — an even more wonderful you. This is the harvest of your pain and suffering.

Hold your head high. Because you have lived with all your might, you are a victor.

LEARNING 4

PURPOSE OF STUDY

What's the point of working so hard at school? What's wrong with having a good time when we're young?

Those questions remind me of a humorous story. A Japanese businessman went to an island in the South Pacific where he found local children relaxing on the beach. He said to them: "Stop idling away your time. Get yourself to school immediately and start studying!"

They replied, "Why should we go to school?"

"If you go to school and study hard," the man said, "you can get good grades."

"Why do we need good grades?" the children asked.

"Ah, if you get good grades, you can get into a good university."

"And what will happen if we get into a good university?"

"If you graduate from a prestigious university, you can work for a big company or serve in a prominent public office. You can also earn a high salary and maybe enter into a good marriage."

"Then what?"

"You can live in a beautiful home and enjoy life."

"And then?"

"You can work very hard, send your kids to a good school and then retire."

"And?" the children queried.

"Then you can go to a nice warm place and spend every day relaxing."

"If that's the goal," the children responded, "then we don't have to wait. We've already achieved it!"

So why do we expend so much time and energy in

studying? For what purpose do we live our lives? What is money for?

If our sole reason for living is to have it easy, there may be no need to make such strenuous efforts to get into a good school or find a good job. Good schools and good jobs do not automatically grant you happiness and ease. Even if you chase after them, there is no guarantee you'll be happy if you get them.

Only by meeting life's challenges can you fulfill your potential and experience true happiness. The purpose of our lives is to fulfill a mission that is ours and ours alone and to do our best to help those who are suffering. To do so, you will need strength and character. That is why I stress constantly how much there is to gain by working hard and challenging yourself now.

When I was a young man, I had a friend who easily excelled in everything and whom everyone admired. So you can imagine my surprise when, twenty-five years later, I received a letter from another friend telling me that this person had ended up leading "a sorrowful life that could only be described as hellish, filled with financial setbacks and family problems."

You may ask how this could happen to someone who had shown such promise in his youth. I believe it was because, having been pampered and fussed over from an early age, my friend never learned what hard work was nor what it meant to struggle to accomplish something. He never learned what a life of genuine depth and substance was. Thinking that everything he desired would just fall in his lap, he never challenged himself, even going out of his way to avoid strenuous effort.

DEMANDS ON TIME

With school, homework, chores and other demands, I have no free time. It's making me feel restricted.

While there's no denying the pressures of one's schedule at times, I believe that to regard the things you mentioned as merely unpleasant demands on your time is an incorrect perspective. If you think about it, it's only because you enjoy great freedom that you have an opportunity to attend school and to study.

Do you look at going to school as a right or as something you're forced to do? As a liberating activity or something that stifles you from doing what you want? It all depends on your personal philosophy, on your wisdom. If you are passive, you'll feel trapped and unhappy in even the freest of environments. But if you take an active approach and challenge your circumstances, you will be free no matter how confining your situation may actually be.

The stronger you are, the freer you will be. Someone without a lot of stamina may have great difficulties climbing even a small hill. Someone sick might not manage it at all. But a strong, healthy person can climb even a mountain easily, with zest and enjoyment. To climb the mountains of your life goals, it's important to develop your strength. Build a strong enough self so that you can be active in school and in your outside activities. If you have strength and capability, you will have freedom.

The same is true of sports or music. To play your chosen sport or instrument with complete mastery and ease, you have to gain an adequate level of proficiency, you have to be prepared to make some sacrifices so you can practice to the degree necessary.

Children who suffer from serious illnesses or who live in war-torn countries often can't go to school even though they may want to. Many children in more fortunate circumstances, who *do* have the opportunity to attend school, never fully appreciate how free they really are. Having the opportunity to go to school — where you can train your life for so much you will want to do in the future — is a sign of the most incredible freedom. And it's a mistake not to realize it.

I'm reminded of a story I recently heard about a young man who had multiple myeloma, a disabling and painful form of bone cancer. In the last two years of his life, with his entire body encased in a cast because of multiple bone fractures, he visited local high schools in his wheelchair to talk about the terrible effects of drug abuse. He would say to the students: "You want to destroy your body with nicotine or alcohol or heroin? You want to smash it up in a car wreck? You're depressed and want to throw yourself off a bridge? Then give me your body! Let me have it! I want it! I'll take it! I want to live!"

During the war in the former Yugoslavia, according to one account, children talked about their dreams. One said, "I had many dreams, but the war is robbing me of all of them." And another said, "Our dream is to live an ordinary life with our friends, to be able to go to school."

In recent years, the African nation of Rwanda has gone through a bitter and cruel civil war. In one family, the children lost both parents; only they and their grandmother survived. One of the older boys had to drop out of school to take care of the rest. He was so sad about not attending school anymore that he often cried through the night. His other siblings still in school would share their lessons with him when he came home from work.

But if that were the whole story, we'd have to conclude that everything depends completely on our environment. That's not the case. Life and the human condition aren't so simple. Buddhism teaches that true freedom is connected to one's inner condition of life. Someone with an expansive life-condition is free even if confined to the most restricted prison on earth.

Natalia Sats, former president of the Moscow State Musical Theater for Children, who fought against oppression and was jailed, also turned her prison cell into a place of learning. She encouraged her fellow prisoners to share their special knowledge with one another. One lectured on chemistry; another taught medicine. Mrs. Sats, who herself was a singer and entertainer, sang songs and recited verses by Aleksandr Pushkin, infusing everyone with courage and hope.

I'm sure you know the story of Helen Keller. At the age of eighteen months, she lost her sight and hearing. Her loss of hearing also made it difficult for her to speak. But by working together with her teacher Anne Sullivan, she eventually learned to read, write and speak, and she graduated from Radcliffe College in Boston.

Surely no one could have been as restricted as she was — unable to speak, hear or see. Her world was one of darkness and silence. But she drove the darkness out of her heart. At the age of nine, she finally spoke her first sentence: "It is warm." She never forgot for the rest of her life the astonishment and joy she experienced at that moment. She had succeeded in breaking out of the prison of silence that confined her.

Being human, however, at times she would feel forlorn

L
E
A
R
N
I
N
G

and disheartened by the long hours she had to spend studying, having all of her textbooks painstakingly spelled into
her hand, while other students were singing and dancing
and enjoying themselves. In *The Story of My Life*, she writes:

> *I slip back many times, I fall, I stand still, I run*
> *against the edge of hidden obstacles, I lose my temper*
> *and find it again and keep it better. I trudge on, I*
> *gain a little, I feel encouraged, I get more eager and*
> *climb higher and begin to see the widening horizon.*
> *Every struggle is a victory.*

DROPPING OUT

I know someone who's dropped out of school, and I'm concerned about what will happen to him.

To be concerned about another's welfare is the mark of an evolved person. There are many ways to express your concern. You could, depending on the situation, let him know that you're worried about him or that you're looking forward to seeing him at school again. You might pay him a visit, write him or give him a call. The situation probably won't change immediately. But simple words like "I'm looking forward to seeing you back at school; it's not the same without you" can make it easier for him to return when he feels ready. In other words, smooth the way for him and make him feel welcome.

A young woman told me she hated her first year of high school because she couldn't make friends. She decided to drop out at the beginning of the second semester because she was miserable, but then a classmate called to cheer her up and invited her to have lunch together at school. Touched and encouraged by the classmate's kindness — and not wanting to let her down — she went to school every day from then on. Now, she says, they are best friends who talk to each other about everything.

There are many reasons, including illness, why people may not attend school. Some people may not wish to pursue traditional educational paths or their situations may prevent them from doing so. One student I know became fed up with high school and found a job that he liked. He is such an excellent worker that he has become invaluable to his employers.

Like him, many people live with a great deal of satisfaction about the choices they've made. And that is fine. I personally hope, however, that you will complete high school and, if possible, college. You can take correspondence courses or go to professional schools or take high school equivalency exams.

But some young people, for various reasons, drop out of school and seek their challenges elsewhere. The important thing for them is to keep moving forward. Each of us is our own person; we shouldn't compare ourselves to others. Keep advancing, even if only by one or two steps, in a way that is true to yourself. Those who live their lives to the fullest, not distracted by the noisy clamor around them, are victors in life. Never give up. Never lose hope.

IMPORTANCE OF GRADES

Even though I've tried hard, I have a pretty low grade-point average. Does this mean I'm a failure?

While getting an education is, of course, important, human potential is not so limited that it can be measured merely by an aptitude for rote learning. Grades are just one means by which to reveal the gem at the center of your life. So I hope you won't evaluate yourself solely on grades or the school you attend.

It has been said recently that one's EQ (emotional quotient) is more important than one's IQ (intelligence quotient). This attests to the importance of such broad-ranging human qualities as compassion or a staunch fighting spirit, which no IQ test can gauge. For this reason, it is foolish to think that your grades at sixteen or eighteen or whatever, will determine the rest of your life. There's much more to human potential than that.

Your studies are, of course, important. But your present grades do not doom you to a less-than-bright future. If you think this way, you will keep yourself from nurturing your abilities. If you give up trying to mine the gem in your life, your personal development will cease. This is something to avoid at all costs.

Some get accepted at universities but don't work hard there. There are some who become overbearing and arrogant. The world needs leaders — not elitists. Others stop striving for personal growth after entering a big company or becoming bureaucrats, doctors or lawyers. Some people who graduate from top universities even resort to crime. Many people, achieving their personal career goals, forget to work for others.

Actually, graduating and getting a job is just the beginning, not the final destination. But many think only about what they want to become, not what they can contribute to society. Greatness as a human being is not determined by educational background or social position.

Your future depends on the efforts you make and whether you are walking the correct path. It's not important how you compare to others but how you compare to who you were yesterday.

The question is how we can live happily, in a way true to ourselves, where we can always look forward and advance. Suppose you are lost in the jungle. You want to find your way out and reach the ocean but don't know which way to go. What do you do? The answer is to keep moving ahead. Eventually, you'll reach a river, and when you follow the river downstream, you will reach the ocean.

Being young means wrestling with all kinds of problems. It means resolving them, in spite of all difficulties, pushing aside the dark clouds of despair and advancing toward the sun, toward hope. Such strength and resilience are the hallmarks of youth.

Buddhists gain the wisdom through daily practice that the important thing is to keep moving forward. While struggling with various problems, it is vital that you advance — even if it's only one or two inches. If you do so, later, when you look back you'll see that you have actually made your way through the jungle in no time.

GETTING INTO A GOOD COLLEGE

Even if you study really hard, it's difficult to get into a good college.

Not attending the college of your choice is certainly disappointing. But, in the long run, graduating from a particular school matters little. Academic background isn't everything; those who start out under difficult circumstances and go on to become people of character can be sources of hope and inspiration for many. The essential point is that you continue to study and learn.

Once you've been accepted by a school — even if it is not your first choice and regardless of how society judges it — it's important for you to decide that the school you are going to is the perfect place for you to learn all you want to learn. This attitude is far more constructive in the long run. And don't allow your confidence to be undermined by the opinions of others.

That having been said, if there's a university you want to get into, then keep studying hard, many times harder than others. Playing and dreaming won't get you what you want. Thinking, "Hanging out with my friends is more important" or "I'm not going to bother with extra-credit work" gets you nowhere. Nothing great is achieved without serious effort. There is no easy road to learning. Study so hard that you surprise everyone. That tremendous effort will become a wonderful, noble, fulfilling memory of your youth. It will be a proud medal of honor.

It is your right as a human being to cherish a dream of what you would like to do — something that is just right for you — and then it is your obligation to continue to challenge yourself to achieve it.

The purpose of study is not which university you attend but to master something that contributes to your self-enrichment. There is a Buddhist saying, "Not to learn is to debase yourself." What makes us human is our capacity to learn.

We are now living in the information age. If you do not continue to study throughout your life, you will soon be left behind. To develop a lifelong study ethic is an important requisite for future leaders. The deadlocks society faces today are in fact the deadlocks of its leaders. And usually the reason for this is that they have stopped learning. They lack the spirit and broad-mindedness to listen to the ideas of the younger generation and to incorporate and implement those that have value.

Education is a lifelong endeavor; graduating from a university isn't enough. Someone once said that we learn only about ten percent of what we need in life from college, no matter how prestigious the school. All of you face the challenge of triumphing in a society that stresses real ability more than ever.

Sometimes it is as simple as the story of the hare and the tortoise. Some people are hares and others, tortoises. Those who win in the end steadily and continuously make their way forward until they reach the finish line. Completing the race is in itself a victory.

FEAR OF FAILURE

I'm afraid of what others think about how I'm doing in school.

The greatest enemy of learning — whether we are studying science, math, art, foreign languages or any other subject — is fear. When we're afraid of being laughed at, of being looked down on by others for our limitations, progress becomes very difficult. We must be brave. So what if others laugh? Anyone who makes fun of people trying their best should be ashamed.

There's no need to compare ourselves to others. What's important is our own growth, even if it is just a little at a time. We should strive constantly to unearth and polish the jewel within ourselves. There are countless examples of people who did not stand out in high school but who struck a rich deposit of hidden potential when they entered society and gained life experience.

L
E
A
R
N
I
N
G

WORK VS. COLLEGE

I think I would rather work and make some money after high school than go on to college.

Whether or not to work after high school is a decision you must make after carefully discussing it with your family. I know many people who have only a high school education and who are now making wonderful contributions to society.

To current high school students, however, I hope you will continue your studies. I strongly encourage you to get a college education. Youth is the ideal time for study. Without a doubt, studying now will prove to be an invaluable asset in life.

When I was a student, Japan was at war. Even though I wanted to study, it was extremely difficult. During the war, studying English was forbidden because it was regarded as an "enemy language." After the war, it was difficult to study, too, as almost all our time was spent making ends meet. Still, I wanted to study, so I went to night school. I hungrily devoured whatever books I could get my hands on. What I learned then has stayed with me, and I use it all the time.

NO MONEY FOR COLLEGE

My family is too poor to send me to college.

I f students from financially strapped families still want to go to college, they can attend their local community two-year program to start the process, go to night school or take correspondence courses — or they can work their way through school, doing part-time jobs. There are also scholarships and special student-loan programs available. Ultimately, it's up to their personal effort.

It is a challenge to work hard and do the best you can every day. The greater the challenge, the greater our exhilaration and sense of accomplishment when we succeed. By doing our best, we can become winners; we can become people of great character. When plants are exposed to strong winds, their roots grow deeper. Everything works this way. Without challenges, we grow lazy and spoiled; our lives become empty and barren. And emptiness means unhappiness.

I hope you won't fall into the trap of being too embarrassed to take out a loan or being afraid of the work required to pay it back. It is people who have no desire to study who are poor. Those filled with enthusiasm for learning are rich.

L
E
A
R
N
I
N
G

VOCATIONAL SCHOOL

My parents want me to go to a university, but I'd rather try something like a vocational school.

You're very lucky to have such parents!

Vocational schools and four-year universities each have their own strong points. In today's society, specialists may have an advantage finding work. But I also think it is wonderful for students to attend a four-year college and then go on to pursue a more specialized field later.

Attending a university and exposing yourself to a wide range of courses is a good way to cultivate your intellect and develop yourself as a person. Higher education is an important tool for building character, too.

Living in a dormitory is itself a lesson in life — a lesson where you learn how to forge ties of friendship and build lasting human relationships.

Highly educated and cultivated individuals throughout the world share a common denominator of broad knowledge and scholarship. Education provides the opportunity to lift yourself to a high level of personal development.

It's like climbing a mountain. The higher you climb, the broader your field of vision and the wider the world unfolds before you. You begin to see things that you could not see before.

At any rate, the question of where you study — at a vocational school, a two-year college or a four-year university — is something only you can decide based on many factors, including your family circumstances, academic ability and personal desires. Of course, in deciding what to do, it is important to consult others — your parents, teachers, friends. But once you make your decision and put it into action, don't look back. You mustn't live your life filled with indecision and lingering regret.

Success or failure in life is decided in the final chapter, not the opening page.

L
E
A
R
N
I
N
G

IMPORTANCE OF READING

I've never been interested in reading.

Many people find reading a chore. Perhaps television leads people away from books. Or maybe computers and video games are more attractive. At any rate, some young people like reading and some don't. But one thing is clear: Those who know the great joys of reading have richer lives and broader perspectives.

Books introduce you to the fragrant flowers of life, to rivers, roads and adventures. You can find stars and light, feel delight or be moved to anger at injustice. You are set adrift on a vast sea of emotion in a ship of reason, moved by the infinite breeze of poetry. Dreams and dramas evolve. The whole world comes alive.

Reading is a privilege only human beings have. No other living thing on this planet can read. Encountering a great book is like encountering a great teacher. Through reading, we come in contact with hundreds and thousands of lives and commune with sages and philosophers from as long as two thousand years ago.

Reading is a journey. You can travel east or west, north and south and discover new people and places.

Reading transcends time. You can go on an expedition with Alexander the Great or make friends with Socrates and Victor Hugo and hold dialogues with them.

Almost without exception, great people throughout history had a book they held dear during their youth — a book that served as a guide, a source of encouragement, a close friend and mentor.

To gain true satisfaction from anything requires practice,

training and effort. You can't become a great skier or skate-boarder without working at it. The same goes for playing the piano or using a computer. Similarly, it takes persever-ance and patience to appreciate reading.

Reading gives you access to the treasures of the human spirit — from all ages and all parts of the world. Someone who knows this possesses unsurpassed wealth. It's like owning countless banks from which you can make unlim-ited withdrawals. And those who have tasted this joy, who look on books as friends, are strong.

L
E
A
R
N
I
N
G

LEARNING TO
ENJOY READING

How can I get myself to enjoy reading more?

The first step is to get into the habit of reading. You can start by finding a book on any topic that interests you. A suspense novel is one good tool to keep yourself reading — the libraries and bookstores are filled with limitless books whose plots, once discoved, will naturally make you want to keep finding out what will happen next. After you've made a selection, take a few spare moments to read each day, maybe while you're riding the bus to school or waiting in line or before going to bed. You will be surprised at how quickly you progress.

Reading is essential to thinking. Perhaps we can even say reading is a sign of our humanity. We mustn't limit our lives to one field to the exclusion of all else. No matter how high people's positions are, if they haven't read great novels by the world's renowned authors, they can never hope to become outstanding leaders. To build a humane society where people live with dignity requires leaders who are acquainted with great literature. This is extremely important.

IMPORTANCE OF HISTORY

Why do we need to study history? History classes are boring with their long lists of facts and dates to memorize.

History is important because it gives us a broader point of view.

Consider this: If we're always looking at the ground when we walk down the street, we're likely to get lost. By looking up and choosing certain landmarks to orient ourselves, we can make sure we are heading in the right direction. Or imagine looking down from a high mountain. From an elevated vantage point, it is easy to pick out the road on which to proceed.

The same is true of life. If you always have a shallow perspective and pay attention only to the minor details at hand, you are sure to get bogged down in petty concerns and never move forward. Even relatively minor hurdles will seem insurmountable. But if you have a broad view of life, you will naturally spot the solution to problems whether they are personal, societal or even those concerning the entire world.

The more problems you have, the more you should read history. Studying history takes you back to the events and lives of people that can shed light on your own life. You meet passionate revolutionaries and despicable traitors, proud tyrants and tragic heroes. You come to know people who sought peaceful lives but were forced to wander through the wilderness. You experience brief moments of peace, like sweet shade from the burning sun, between seemingly endless stretches of war.

By studying history you see large numbers of people

LEARNING

sacrificed for what we now know was foolish superstition, as well as men and women of principle who gave their lives out of love for their contemporaries. You meet great people who pulled themselves up from the depths of suffering to make the impossible possible. You can watch this drama from a distance or view it as though you were in its midst. Watching it unfold in your mind, you naturally learn to see life from an expansive point of view. You can see yourself riding the crest of the grand river of history. We see where we have come from, where we are and where we're going.

To know history is to know oneself. The better we know ourselves and human nature, the more accurate a picture we get of history. From a Buddhist perspective, history is a record of human tendencies, of cause and effect. It is the science of human activity, the statistics of the human race.

For instance, though we can't predict the weather with complete accuracy, we can forecast trends based on probability and statistics. The human heart is also unpredictable, but history allows us to see trends and statistics that give us insight into the future.

The study of history, then, is the study of humanity. History is a mirror that guides us in shaping the future. Youth are the protagonists who will write the fresh history of tomorrow. You need a mirror to see your own face. Similarly, armed with the mirror of history, you can see what needs to be done in the world around you.

My mentor, Josei Toda, taught that history is a signpost to help us move with greater certainty from past to present, from present to future, toward our goals of peace and the harmonious coexistence of all humanity.

Since there is such an abundance of recorded history, one person cannot be expected to absorb it all. What's essential is to gain a firm historical perspective, an understanding of basic historical principles. If we can learn, by studying history, about humanity's negative tendencies, we can be on the lookout for them and avoid a repetition of our dark, destructive past. Repeating history's abominations means we have failed to learn history's lessons. As the philosopher George Santayana said, "Those who cannot remember the past are condemned to repeat it."

L
E
A
R
N
I
N
G

TRUTH AND HISTORY

The more I study history, the more I find out what I'd been taught isn't true.

History is not definitive. It can be interpreted in many ways, which is why we mustn't blindly trust what we read in history books. Napoleon described history as an agreed-upon story. That is true in some respects — history is written from a specific perspective and does not reflect the absolute, objective truth.

Of course, we know the dates of certain events; those are unarguable facts. But the historical conclusions based on those dates are not so reliable. At times, the exact opposite of the truth becomes the prevailing historical opinion. And far more important truths are not recorded at all.

For example, let's look at the Crusades, which were launched by European Christians against the Islamic powers during the Middle Ages. European and Islamic accounts of the Crusades have almost nothing in common! Naturally, Islamic history books don't use the heroic-sounding term *crusaders* but describe those who invaded their lands as aggressors.

In fact, at the time of the Crusades, Islamic civilization was far more advanced than Europe's. The Crusaders invaded Islamic lands, looting and pillaging, leaving behind a trail of destruction. Islamic histories record the horrible atrocities that the crusaders committed.

Learning about the Crusades is not simply a matter of understanding the past, either. Prejudice and animosity between Christian and Islamic cultures persist today, casting a dark shadow over our chances for world peace. It is today's problem. It is a problem for the future.

Another example: Not very long ago, it was widely taught that Christopher Columbus discovered the Americas. But people were already living there. The discovery was solely from the European perspective. The problem is that the concept of discovery inherently demeans the Americas' original inhabitants. Some conquerors of the so-called New World didn't even regard the indigenous peoples as human beings!

As Europeans moved from one Caribbean island to another, they slaughtered the inhabitants or rounded them up for slave labor and nearly wiped out entire populations. The native inhabitants had welcomed them with open arms and the European invaders repaid them with violence. What can we say about this "historical truth"? The view that Columbus discovered America legitimizes the "discoverers" and therefore legitimizes similar actions by others. Within the word *discovery* is a self-righteous historical view, a view of humanity that all too often justifies the subjugation of other peoples in the conquerors' interests.

This is called the colonial viewpoint, which spawned numerous tragedies throughout the world since the dawn of time. This is why understanding history is important. Humanity's history of "discovery" became a future of domination leading to misery and tragedy.

This narrow colonial view of history lay behind Japan's invasion of Asia. From the Meiji period, beginning in 1868, we Japanese were intent on catching up with Europe and aimed at becoming the Europeans of Asia. We mistreated our fellow Asians in the same way that Europeans treated the indigenous peoples of America after Columbus's arrival. We became subservient and fawning to white people while arrogant and cruel to all other races.

LEARNING

What we should have done, of course, was build friendly ties with our fellow Asians and work with them toward world peace. If Japanese leaders had possessed that view — and vision of the future — Japan's recent history would have been entirely different.

So, you see, a single historical event can assume different meanings depending upon how it is interpreted, depending on which side you are on. Both images may appear equally valid, but the truth lies somewhere in between.

ART TRANSFORMS THE HEART

I've been told art is important, but art appreciation classes seem very stuffy and intimidating.

Formal instruction in art can seem that way, it's true. But surely no one regards a bird's song as formal or frightening. Nor I'm sure does anyone feel intimidated by gazing at a meadow of flowers. Who can fail to be captivated by the beauty of cherry blossoms in full bloom in the moonlight? And on a glorious day, we all look up at the blue sky and think, "How wonderful!" The bubbling of a stream delights the ear, refreshing our senses. These are all examples of our intuitive love of beauty.

Art is beauty. Great works of art, just like the beauty inherent in nature, are a balm for the spirit — a source of vitality. Art should calm and soothe us, not put us on the defensive or make us uncomfortable. It can encourage us when we are run-down, lift our spirits when we are tense.

Many of our daily activities are filled with art and culture. For instance, when we try to look our best or make a dirty room spotless, we are striving to create beauty. A single flower in a vase can completely transform a room, giving it a warm, gentle touch. Such is the power of beauty.

Art is the liberation of the humanity inside you.

Institutions treat us as parts in a machine. They assign us ranks and place considerable pressure on us to fulfill our defined roles. We need something to help us restore our lost or distorted humanity. Each of us has suppressed feelings that have built up, a voiceless cry in the depths of our souls, waiting for expression. Art, both in practice and appreciation, gives those feelings voice and form.

L E A R N I N G

Letting those feelings out through the pursuit of pleasure may suffice for a while. But in the long run such distractions bring no true satisfaction, because our true selves, our true heart's desires, have not been set free. Art is the cry of the soul from the depths of one's being.

When we create or appreciate art, we set free the spirit trapped within. That is why art arouses such joy. Art — whether skillfully executed or not — is the emotion, the pleasure of expressing life as it is. Those who see art are moved by its passion and strength, its intensity and beauty. That is why it is impossible to separate life from art. Political and economic developments may seem to dominate the news, but culture and education are the forces that actually shape an age, since they transform the human heart.

The Buddhist concept of cherry, plum, peach and damson — the idea that each person should live earnestly, true to his or her unique individuality — has a lot in common with culture and art. Culture is the flowering of each individual's true humanity, which is why it transcends national boundaries, time periods and other distinctions. Likewise, one result of Buddhist practice is that we can lead a truly cultured life and serve as an inspiration to others.

APPRECIATING ART

Can I learn to appreciate art even without classes?

Sure. You can begin by simply enjoying art. That is the most important first step. View good paintings. Listen to good music. Experiencing fine art will develop and nurture your mind.

Know this: If you start out with a scholarly or analytical approach, you're likely to end up confused about what art really is. I doubt very much that people listening to a bird's song or gazing at a meadow covered with flowers analyze it.

A great work of art is one that inspires you. When you experience it, you yourself are moved. Don't look at art through the eyes of others. Don't listen to music with someone else's ears. React to a work of art with your own feelings, your own heart and mind. If you allow yourself to be swayed by the opinions of others — "It must be good, because everyone else likes it," "It must be bad, because no one else likes it" — your feelings, your sensibilities, which are the very core of the artistic experience, will wither and die.

Enjoying art to the fullest requires that you abandon all preconceived notions. Confront the work directly, with your entire being. If you are deeply moved, then that work is, for you, a great work of art.

Great works of art are universal. They are alive, endowed with the creator's powerful life force and spirit. The renowned French sculptor Auguste Rodin, who worked in the late 1800s, said that the important thing for artists is "to feel, to love, to hope, to tremble, to live. It is to be, before an artist, a human being." These human feelings — hope, love, anger, fear — are communicated to us through the artist's work. The vibrations of the artist's spirit set off similar vibrations within our own hearts. This is the essential experience of art. It is a shared feeling that links the creator and the viewer, transcending boundaries of time and space.

Of course, to fully appreciate some great works of art, we need to concentrate. But appreciation starts with simply experiencing the work. With music, for instance, we start by listening. With a painting, we start by looking. With literature, we start by reading. Too many people, I'm afraid, are so intent on analyzing art that they don't really see it.

Probably the best way is to see or hear as many of the generally agreed-upon masterpieces of world art as you can, which will cultivate and refine your sensibilities. You will naturally learn to distinguish good from bad.

Looking at second- and third-rate art will not help you understand first-rate art, but it will teach you the distinction. Your critical eye will emerge. That is why you should make an effort to experience the best from the very start.

You can see great art in books, of course, but seeing the real thing is entirely different. It's the difference between seeing a photograph of someone and the actual person. True art, true culture, enriches the individual, encourages self-expression and brings joy and happiness to people regardless of their fame or wealth. Genuine art and culture foster that spirit, they enrich our lives and make them truly worth living. Therefore, it would be great if you can find time to take classes — both in art appreciation and in making art — because they can enhance us as individuals.

5

WORK

- Choosing a Career

- Finding Your Mission

- Talent

- The Right Job

- Changing Careers

- Not Working

- Making Money

- Working for a Cause

CHOOSING A CAREER

I'm confused about what career to pursue.

The Japanese poet Takuboku Ishikawa, who wrote at the turn of the twentieth century, once penned this verse, which I recorded in my journal when I was young:

> *Would that I had a vocation*
> *To carry out with joy.*
> *Once I have fulfilled it*
> *I wish to die.*

W
O
R
K

He is talking about his mission, the work for which he was born. Few people, however, are fortunate enough to know their mission from the outset. I often hear students say things like: "My parents want me to become a doctor, but I'm not sure it's what I want to do," or "I wanted to be a journalist but don't think I have what it takes," or "My choices are limited because of the subjects I've taken," or "I'm not interested in anything in particular, but I'd like to be famous," or "My dreams keep changing with every new person I meet." Some have also said to me, "I get scared sometimes because I have no idea what I want to do in the future."

Well, life is long. The true result of your daily struggles to find your mission may not be revealed to you until your forties, fifties and sixties. So it is important that you each find something — it doesn't matter what — with which to challenge yourself while you are young. Regard your youth as the time to study and train yourself.

Everyone has a unique mission — or purpose — that

only he or she can fulfill. That doesn't mean, however, that you should sit around and do nothing, waiting for the answer to come to you or for someone to tell you what it is. By challenging yourself, you will finally discover your mission on your own.

You are like a mountain concealing a precious gem. Precious gems start out buried underground. If they are not mined, they'll stay buried. And if they aren't polished once they've been dug out, they will remain forever in the rough. What a shame it would be to end your life without having uncovered your inner jewel. So when parents or teachers tell you to study hard, they are saying in effect, by plunging into any area that interests you, you can unearth the jewel in your life and find satisfaction in making it sparkle.

Tenacity is crucial. You cannot make the gem inside you shine with halfhearted efforts.

You have the right to decide what type of job you want to do; the choices are open. Having said that, however, many jobs require a certain level of academic qualification and experience. Some people start working right out of high school, either by choice or because of their family situation. Others join the work force after graduating from college, while others become homemakers. Some people aim to become public servants, and still others strive to gain technical proficiency in some field. The bottom line is that there are many options, all of which you are at liberty to choose from.

If you can't decide what kind of work you'd like to do, why not start out with a job you can get easily, something you are familiar with? That way you can gain practical experience and find out what you're good at. In any case, don't worry.

Getting a job is just the starting point in uncovering

your true ability; it is absolutely not the final goal. There is no need to be impatient. It is important that you make your way up the mountain of life steadily, without rushing or giving up.

When you decide what you want to do in the future, forge ahead purposefully. Do not be halfhearted. When you pursue something with strong determination, you will have no regrets even should you fail. And if you succeed, you can achieve truly great things. Whether you fail or succeed, your steady efforts will lead you to your next path.

W
O
R
K

FINDING YOUR MISSION

How do I discover my mission in life?

First, I want to repeat that you won't find it by standing still. What's important is that you challenge yourself in something, it doesn't matter what. Then by making consistent effort, the direction you should take will open up before you naturally. It's important, therefore, to have the courage to ask yourself what you should be doing now, this very moment.

The key, in other words, is to climb the mountain that is right before you. As you ascend its slopes, you will develop your muscles, increasing your strength and endurance. Such training will enable you to challenge still higher mountains. It is vital that you continue making such efforts.

Climb the mountain in front of you. When you reach the summit, wide new horizons will stretch out before you. Little by little, you will understand your mission.

Those who remember they have a unique mission are the strong ones. Whatever their problems, they will never be defeated. They can transform all of their problems into catalysts for growth toward a hope-filled future.

Life is about scaling one mountain, then facing the next one, followed by the one after that. Those who persevere and finally succeed in conquering the highest mountain are victors in life. On the other hand, those who avoid such challenges and take the easy route, descending into the valleys, will end in defeat. To put it simply, we have two choices in life: We can either climb the mountain before us or descend into the valley.

TALENT

I feel ordinary, like I have no special abilities or talents.

That just isn't true. The problem lies in people limiting themselves. Everyone has some kind of gift. Being talented doesn't just mean being a good musician, writer or athlete — there are many kinds of talent. For instance, you may be a great conversationalist or make friends easily or put others at ease. Or you may have a gift for nursing, a knack for telling jokes, selling things or economizing. You may be always punctual, patient, reliable, kind or optimistic. You may love new challenges or be strongly committed to peace or to bringing joy to others.

As Nichiren taught, each of us is as unique as a cherry blossom, plum blossom, peach blossom or damson blossom. Each blossom is distinctly wondrous; accordingly, each blooms in the way that only it can.

Without a doubt each person has an innate talent. The question is: How do you discover that talent? The only way is to exert yourself to the limit in whatever is before you. Your true potential will emerge when you give everything you've got to your studies, sports, extracurricular activities or whatever you are engaged in.

The important thing is that you get into the habit of challenging yourself to the limit. In a sense, the results you get are not so important. The actual grades you receive in high school, for instance, won't decide the rest of your life. But the habit of pushing yourself to the limit will in time bear fruit. It will distinguish you from others without fail. It will bring your unique talent to shine.

W
O
R
K

THE RIGHT JOB

What should I look for when trying to find the right job?

Tsunesaburo Makiguchi, the first president of the Soka Gakkai, taught that there are three kinds of value: beauty, benefit and good. In the working world, to find a job you like corresponds to the value of beauty; to get a job that earns a salary that can support your daily life corresponds to the value of benefit; and the value of good means finding a job that helps others and contributes to society.

Not many can find the perfect job from the start. Some may have a job they like, but it doesn't put food on the table; or their job may pay well, but they hate it. That's the way things go sometimes. Also, some discover that they're just not cut out for the career they had dreamed of.

My mentor, Josei Toda, emphasized the importance of first becoming indispensable wherever you are. Instead of moaning that a job falls short of what you'd like to be doing, he said, become a first-class individual at that job. This will open the path leading to your next phase in life, during which you should also continue doing your best. Such continuous efforts are guaranteed to land you a job that you like, that supports your life, and that allows you to contribute to society.

Then, when you look back later, you will see how all your past efforts have become precious assets in your ideal field. You will realize that none of your efforts and hardships have been wasted.

CHANGING CAREERS

What if you start following one dream but have a change of heart and want to pursue a different path?

That's perfectly all right. Few people end up doing what they planned or dreamed of doing in the beginning.

In my case, I wanted to be a newspaper reporter, but my poor health prevented me from pursuing that profession. Today, however, I have become a writer.

At one point, I worked for a small publishing company. Because of its small staff, I had to work very hard — but, because of that, I gained a great deal of practical experience.

After the war, I worked for another small operation, but what I went through on that job gave me a chance to really look at myself. Everything I learned back then is of value to my life now. The important thing is to develop yourself in your present situation and to take control of your growth.

Once you have decided on a job, I hope you will not be the kind of person who quits at the drop of a hat or is always insecure and complaining. Nevertheless, if after you've given it your all, you decide that your job isn't right for you and you move on, that's all right, too.

Taking your place as a member of society is a challenge; it is a struggle to survive. But wherever you are is exactly where you need to be, so strive there to the best of your ability.

A tree doesn't grow strong and tall within one or two days. In the same way, successful people didn't become successful in only a few years. This applies to everything.

W
O
R
K

NOT WORKING

Given the choice, I'd rather not have to work at all.

Some view work as an unpleasant chore they must do to earn money to support their leisure activities. But in the words of a character from *The Lower Depths*, by Maxim Gorky: "When work is a pleasure, life is a joy! When work is a duty, life is slavery." Your attitude toward work — even your college class work, which may take up the better part of your day — decisively determines your quality of life.

A friend of mine, the late philosophy professor David Norton, once said:

> *Many students are caught up in the notion that the only purpose of employment is to earn money, that happiness means having money to gratify their desires. But since there is no limit to those desires, they can never truly be satisfied. Real happiness is found in work itself. Through work, one can develop and fulfill oneself and bring forth the unique value that lies within — and share that value with society. Work exists for the joy of creating value.*

It is just as he says. A person's work should bring happiness to others. Life is truly wonderful when you're needed somewhere. How boring and empty life would be if just because we had the means, all we did every day was pursue idle diversions.

MAKING MONEY

How concerned should I be with salary?

Especially for young people, it's important not to be overly concerned with salary. Along with doing your best where you are, it is best to have the spirit, "I'll do more than I'm paid for!" This is how you can train yourself.

To slack off at work just because the salary isn't generous is foolish. To receive a salary — anything earned through honest labor — is precious, regardless of the amount.

Of course, it is satisfying to receive a good salary, but $100 earned through one's hard work and efforts is a golden treasure — whereas stealing that same $100 or acquiring it through other illicit means has no more value than dung or rubble. Stolen or extorted money is dirty. It will not bring happiness. As the saying goes, "Ill gotten, ill spent." Influential government officials who once enjoyed great prestige but who have been caught accepting bribes must live the rest of their lives labeled as criminals.

Ultimately, the greatest happiness is found in applying yourself with confidence and wisdom in your workplace as an exemplary member of society, working hard to achieve a fulfilling life and the well-being of your family. Those who do so are victors in life.

W
O
R
K

WORKING FOR A CAUSE

Is working for a good cause better than just having some job?

Aspiring to devote yourself to a humane cause, to uphold human rights and act on your desire to work for the happiness and welfare of others, is a truly laudable ambition.

In no way does that mean, however, that you cannot contribute to peace and to the betterment of society unless you are in some special profession or organization. While I highly commend anyone who works for a charity or becomes a volunteer worker, there are many people striving for peace in their own humble specialties.

I have met many such people, like Rosa Parks, the mother of the American civil rights movement, who was working as a department store tailor's assistant when she became the catalyst for the famous bus boycott in Montgomery, Alabama, in 1955; and Argentina's Adolfo Pérez Esquivel, a sculptor and architect, who won the Nobel Peace Prize for his activities to protect human rights.

The main thing is to be proud of the work you do, to live true to yourself. Activity is another name for happiness. What's important is that you give free, unfettered play to your unique talents, that you live with the full radiance of your being. This is what it means to be truly alive.

DREAMS 6 & GOALS

- Big Dreams

- Gaining Focus

- Being Smart Enough

- Following Your Heart

- Never Giving Up

- Strengthening Your Resolve

- Importance of Courage

- Courage and Compassion

BIG DREAMS

My dreams sometimes seem impossible to achieve.

That's understandable. My mentor, Mr. Toda, once told me: "It's perfectly all right for youth to cherish dreams that may seem almost too big. What we can achieve in a single lifetime is always but a fraction of what we would like to achieve. So if you start out with expectations that are too low, you may end up not accomplishing anything at all."

Of course, if you make no efforts, your dreams will amount to nothing but sheer fantasy. Effort, hard work, *that* is the bridge that connects your dreams to reality. Those who make steady efforts are filled with hope. And hope, in turn, arises from steady efforts. Embrace your dreams and advance as far as they can carry you. Start now while you are young.

D
R
E
A
M
S
&
G
O
A
L
S

GAINING FOCUS

I'm not sure what I want to do with my life. How do I get more focused?

Although it is natural to be unsure about your future, it's crucial that you try to accomplish something — *anything*. The thought of that might seem overwhelming. But as the ancient saying goes, "The journey of a thousand miles begins with a single step." Discovering our goals and dreams begins with the first step of deciding to find them. From there, we proceed step by step — in steady increments through daily efforts.

The track star Emil Zatopek of Czechoslovakia, who won the 1952 Olympic men's marathon, found his training so excruciating at times that he would tell himself, "I'll just try to make it to the next telephone pole." Then, when he reached it, he would say to himself again, "OK, I'll just go as far as the next one," and push himself a little further. These persistent efforts to keep challenging himself ultimately led to his victory.

The practice of Buddhism automatically entails steady, daily advancement. Each morning and evening, practitioners of Nichiren's Buddhism renew their determination through chanting Nam-myoho-renge-kyo. Among its many benefits, our chant brings about a robust life force, enabling us to tackle all that life puts before us, even if we had felt defeated beforehand.

So do something! Start something! As you make consistent efforts, you will begin to see your goals come into focus. You will discover your mission — the one only you can fulfill.

For example, it is important to develop skills in areas you enjoy. The key is to have something in which you can take pride, something you are willing to challenge. It might be excelling in math, a foreign language, a sport, an extracurricular activity, making friends or doing volunteer work. The people around you may know you better in some ways than you do yourself, so if you summon up the courage to ask them for advice, you might find the doors to new possibilities opening unexpectedly.

A person who has firm goals is way ahead of a person who has none. Setting goals is the starting point from which you begin to construct your life. Even if your goals change as you go along, they are no less important. Youth is the time to struggle to develop and shape yourself, an ongoing challenge to train spiritually, intellectually and physically.

A solid foundation is essential in all things. No building can stand without a foundation. The same is true in life. And the time to construct that foundation is now, during your youth. As the French writer Romain Rolland noted, a pyramid cannot be built from the top down.

D
R
E
A
M
S
&
G
O
A
L
S

BEING SMART ENOUGH

What if I am not smart enough to achieve my dreams?

It has been said that at most we use only about half our brain cells during our lifetime. Some scholars even maintain that we use less than ten percent of them. In other words, hardly anyone is using his or her brain to its fullest potential.

I have also heard that the brain continues to grow until our early twenties. In that respect, how much we develop our intellect before age twenty or so will greatly affect the rest of our lives — which underscores the importance of our teenage years.

Of course, your entire future does not hinge on your grades at school, nor do good grades automatically guarantee happiness or poor grades unhappiness.

You mustn't put yourself down or sell yourself short. Human potential is a funny thing. If you tell yourself that you're not smart, your brain really does grow sluggish. Instead, tell yourself with conviction: "My brain's asleep because I'm hardly using it. So if I just make some effort, I can do anything." This is, in fact, the truth. The more you use your brain, the brighter you will become.

FOLLOWING YOUR HEART

Sometimes I get confused between what other people want for me and what I want for myself.

M any times parents or well-meaning friends may try to persuade you to set a goal you do not feel comfortable with. Though they may have your best interests in mind — and it is important to thank them and consider what they say — you must listen to your own heart.

What matters most is the extent to which you can realize your potential and how much you can contribute to others' happiness. To do this, you have to forge a solid sense of identity. You need to build your foundation and become strong.

You may say you want a happy family, but happiness is not handed to you on a platter. You will become happy only to the extent that you develop a strong inner core. You may say that you want to be a kind person, but to exhibit true kindness requires that you be strong.

It is important to savor the joy that comes from living with fresh and constantly growing aspirations as you strive to realize the dreams and goals you have resolved to pursue. In other words, we become our best selves when pursuing a goal that allows us to fully develop and make use of our uniqueness.

We can lead fulfilling lives when we work toward a great goal. Indian political and spiritual leader Mahatma Gandhi is an excellent example. As a boy, Gandhi was excruciatingly shy. He was unable to sleep without a light on, haunted by imaginary thieves, ghosts and serpents. Introverted, always worried people would make fun of him,

D
R
E
A
M
S
&
G
O
A
L
S

he struggled this way for many years and had many personal setbacks. And yet, as we have come to know, Gandhi went on to become the great leader of nationalist India and the global symbol for achieving peace through nonviolent means.

NEVER GIVING UP

It's so hard to keep going sometimes when I hit so many obstacles.

Having big dreams can prevent you from being swayed by minor bumps in the road. Even if you suffer a setback, as long as you can keep your goals in sight you have reasons not to give up. Forge on, even if at times you feel, "I can't go any further."

What is defeat in life? It is not merely making a mistake; defeat means giving up on yourself in the midst of difficulty. What is true success in life? True success means winning in your battle with yourself. Those who persist in the pursuit of their dreams, no matter what the hurdles, are winners in life, for they have won over their weaknesses.

Refusing to stand up means you are defeated. True victors are those who stand up each time they fall down.

My friend Orlando Cepeda was a well-known major league baseball player for many years, playing mainly with the San Francisco Giants. In 1958, he was the National League Rookie of the Year, and in 1967, National League MVP. He hit a career total of 379 home runs and was elected to play in the all-star game eleven times. He was one of the most feared batters in the major leagues in the 1960s. Everybody thought he would easily make the Hall of Fame. But after he retired from baseball, things took a turn for the worse. He was arrested for possession of drugs.

You can't gain entry into the Hall of Fame just by having a superb baseball record. Your integrity as a human being is also examined in the process of nomination and election. After Orlando's arrest, he was largely ignored by

DREAMS & GOALS

the Hall of Fame selection board.

In 1982, a friend introduced him to the practice of Nichiren Buddhism. A new challenge took root in his life as he learned to never give up on his dreams. He devoted himself not only to changing his own life for the better but also to helping young people start their lives afresh. He never lost his cherished desire to make it to the Hall of Fame, but the reason behind it changed. He wanted to make it into the Hall as an example to encourage others to better their lives. Orlando made many friends and developed a career with the Giants as a sort of goodwill ambassador, especially encouraging many young players of Latin descent. His relentless efforts to improve his life were acknowledged by the Hall of Fame Committee on Veterans — a group of mostly retired sportswriters, ballplayers and team executives — and in 1999 he was triumphantly inducted into the Hall.

NEVER GIVING UP

What can I say to my friends who give up when facing a problem?

First, you can encourage them that if they know what the problem is, they are halfway toward solving it!

People tend to lack willpower. To take the path of least resistance is human nature. One technique you can suggest to those short on willpower or self-motivation is to focus on one task at a time — it can be anything — and keep at it until they're absolutely satisfied they've done their best. Taking the first step leads to the next one.

Life is an everlasting struggle with ourselves. It is a tug of war between moving forward and regressing, between happiness and unhappiness. Outstanding individuals didn't become great overnight. They disciplined themselves to overcome their weaknesses, to conquer their lack of caring and motivation until they became true victors in life. One reason Buddhists chant Nam-myoho-renge-kyo each day is to develop strong will and discipline and, along with those, the ability to tackle any problem seriously and with the determination to overcome it.

DREAMS & GOALS

STRENGTHENING
YOUR RESOLVE

I feel my determination and willingness to work hard getting weaker.

Anyone who has ever made a resolution discovers that the strength of that determination fades with time. The moment you feel your determination flagging, make a new determination. Tell yourself: "OK, I will start again from now!" If you fall down seven times, get up for an eighth go at it. Don't give up when you feel discouraged — just pick yourself up and renew your determination each time.

Our resolve may waver sometimes, but what's important is that we don't become discouraged and throw in the towel when it does. Realizing that we've become lazy is evidence we are growing.

IMPORTANCE OF COURAGE

Sometimes I'm afraid to go after what I want.

Courage is very important. Whether or not we have courage has a crucial bearing on the direction of our lives. People who have courage are happy.

Speaking out to a friend you feel has made a mistake, helping someone in need, even asking questions in class — these may seem like trifling concerns, but they're very serious. Small things matter. What may look like a small act of courage is courage nevertheless. The important thing is to be willing to take a step forward.

Young people have problems, just as adults have. As long as we're alive, we'll face all kinds of problems. But no matter what happens, we simply have to live with courage and press on, aiming always toward the future. No one can escape the realities of daily life. Life and the world we live in are like a storm-tossed sea; we have to make our way through it, buffeted by all kinds of experiences. This is part of our inescapable human destiny.

All of us have our own hopes and dreams, our own way of life, our own ideals and joys, our own sufferings, pain and grief. No matter how wonderful our dreams, how noble our ideals, or how high our hopes, ultimately we need courage to make them a reality in the face of sufferings and hurdles. No matter what happens, we have to get on with life and keep working toward our ideals and dreams. Our greatest ideas or plans, our boundless compassion for others — all of these will come to nothing unless we have the courage to put them into action. Without action, it's as if they never existed.

The courageous have the strength to forge ahead,

calmly traversing life's ups and downs and advancing steadily toward the summit of their chosen goals and dreams. Courage is a powerful asset. Those who lack courage stray from the correct path and succumb to apathy, negativity and destructive ways. They run away from hardship, seeking only to live lives of ease and comfort. Consequently, those who lack courage cannot devote themselves to the happiness of others, nor can they improve themselves or achieve anything important or lasting. It's as if their engine has suffered a malfunction.

The German poet Goethe declared that the loss of possessions and reputation is insignificant because you can always set out to restore them, whereas the loss of courage is the loss of everything. In a poem titled "Zahme Xenien [VIII]," he writes:

> *Possessions lost — little lost!*
> *Just reflect on yourself*
> *And acquire new ones.*
> *Honor lost — much lost!*
> *Just gain a good reputation*
> *And people will change their minds.*
> *Courage lost — all lost!*
> *It would have been better never to have been born.*

If you summon your courage to challenge something, you'll never regret it. How sad it would be to spend your life wishing, "If only I'd had a little more courage." Whatever the outcome, the important thing is to take a step forward on the path that you believe is right. There's no need to worry about what others may think. It's your life, after all. Be true to yourself.

The eighteenth-century German philosopher and poet

Friedrich Schiller said, "Those who are strong when they stand alone possess true courage." I have treasured those words since I was young.

It is wrong to blindly follow the crowd. Going along with something without any real thought, just because everyone is doing it, leads to mental laziness and apathy. And that's dangerous.

We mustn't be led astray. We must never give up our commitment to peace, our desire to learn and our love for humanity. Putting those ideals into practice and spreading them among others is an act of courage. Courage lies inside us. We have to summon it from the depths of our lives.

COURAGE AND COMPASSION

What exactly is courage?

We can find courage in many areas of human endeavor, such as the courage to take part in an adventure or the courage to excel at sports, but this is only one aspect of courage. Performing reckless stunts or being a fighter is a very different type of courage than we're talking about. A show of bravado may seem like courage, but it has no moral grounding. Physical violence lacks intelligence, the consideration for others and the spirit of cooperation that are essential to all human beings. It is completely alien to what human beings should strive for.

Courage is the strength to live our lives the right way, to walk the right path. It can take many forms — for example, thinking about the best way for your country and the world to achieve peace and then taking action to make that happen. That is the courage born of conviction. Or thinking about what you can do to contribute to people's happiness and then working constructively toward that goal. That is the courage of love for humanity. As a parent or a schoolteacher, for example, discovering what you can do for the children in your care and then doing it, or thinking about how you can help and support your friends and following through — that is the unpretentious courage of daily life.

The most important kind of courage is the courage required to live a good life each day. For example, the courage to study hard or to form and sustain good, solid friendships — this kind of courage we might even call perseverance, a virtue that directs our lives in a positive direction. This type of courage may not be flashy, but it is truly the most important.

The people in the spotlight, the people who always seem to be doing big, important things, are not always courageous. And it goes without saying that war and oppression are not acts of courage but of cowardice.

Those who have *no* courage are the ones who steal, who oppress, who kill and maim, who threaten people with weapons, who wage war. People do such evil things because they are cowards. Cowardice is dangerous. True courage means carrying out just and beneficial activities; it means living honestly. This is the most priceless sort of courage.

Essentially, courage is a matter of perseverance. A mother's desire to raise her children to become fine adults, no matter how hard she has to work to do it, is a very noble form of courage. The other side of courage is compassion. They're two sides of the same coin. True courage is always backed by compassion; there is nothing evil or malicious behind it. If there is any ill intention, you can be sure it is not real courage. A mother's feeling for her children is a perfect example of courage and compassion.

And in fact, if we act with courage, we find that our compassion for others actually grows deeper. Courage is the ultimate virtue to strive for.

DREAMS & GOALS

CONFIDENCE 7

- Maintaining Hope

- True Potential

- Facing Up to Problems

- Bring Out Your Best

- Nature vs. Nurture

- Changing Karma

- Seeing Beyond Faults

- Handling Criticism

- Shyness

- Self-consciousness

- Viewing Others Positively

MAINTAINING HOPE

Sometimes I feel so hopeless and pessimistic. What can I do to increase my self-confidence?

First, please understand, life is long! The way things are now will not last forever. Even if you have problems, even if you have made mistakes or have done things you regret, your whole future still lies ahead of you. Don't worry endlessly over every obstacle or problem. Above all, do not despair or be defeated by your impatience.

Nothing is hopeless. The worst mistake you can make when young is to give up on a dream, to not challenge yourself for fear of failure. The past is the past and the future is the future. Keep moving forward with a steady eye on what is ahead, telling yourself: "I'll start from today!" "I'll start fresh from this moment!" This spirit — starting from the present moment — is at the heart of Buddhist philosophy.

Happiness in life does not depend on how well things go in your youth. No matter how many mistakes you make, you always have another chance. Be ambitious and keep striving toward the future. If you're not happy with your achievements in high school, then give it your all at college. If that's not to your satisfaction, there's still hope after graduation as you challenge yourself as an active member of society. True success in life does not reveal itself until we reach our forties or fifties. If you experience setbacks along the way, continue with a fighting spirit into your forties, fifties, sixties and seventies.

My experience after more than seventy years of life has taught me to clearly recognize the human patterns that determine victory or defeat.

CONFIDENCE

Many of the most famous people in our history appeared far from outstanding in their youth. Winston Churchill was well known for his many failures at school. Mahatma Gandhi wasn't a remarkable student, either; he was shy, timid and a poor speaker.

So don't be too hard on yourself. You are still young — a work in progress and still developing. To be growing and improving are wonderful things. Just continue to press on tenaciously to find your way forward despite the suffering and pain that are part of youth and growing up. Indeed, that's the only way to grow.

It is important not to lose hope. Losing hope is, in a way, like living in a winter of the spirit. The English Romantic poet Shelley said, "If Winter comes, can Spring be far behind?" No matter how long and bitter the winter may be, spring always follows. This is the law of the universe, the law of life.

The same applies to us. If we seem to be weathering an endless winter, we mustn't abandon hope. As long as we have hope, spring is near. It will come without fail.

Spring is a time of blossoming. Buddhism teaches that all things have a unique beauty and a unique unfolding. Every person has a singular mission, his or her individuality and way of living. It's important to recognize that truth and respect it. That is the natural order of things. That is how it works in the world of flowers — and in the world of human beings, different kinds of flowers bloom harmoniously in beautiful profusion.

TRUE POTENTIAL

I often end up comparing myself to others and feeling discouraged.

Yes, young people often fall into this habit. But I cannot say this too strongly: Do not allow yourself to compare yourself to others! Be true to who you are and continue to learn with all your might. Even if you are ridiculed, even if you suffer disappointments and setbacks, continue to advance and do not be defeated. When you muster this strong determination in your heart, you are already halfway to victory. Rather than comparing your every joy and sorrow to that of others, aim to surpass your limits in your current situation. Those who can accomplish this throughout life are the true victors, the true geniuses.

When you hold fast to your beliefs and live true to yourself, your real value as a human being shines through. Buddhism teaches the concept of 'realizing your inherent potential.' It refers to your most refined individuality. In other words, it means manifesting your true nature and bringing it forward to illuminate all around you.

C O N F I D E N C E

FACING UP TO PROBLEMS

When I face problems, running away sometimes seems like the easiest solution.

You *can* run away, of course. That freedom exists. But it is a very small, petty freedom. It only leads to a life of great hardship, a life in which you will be powerless, weak and completely frustrated.

Alongside this small freedom, however, exists a much greater freedom. The Japanese novelist Eiji Yoshikawa writes, "Great character is forged through hardship." Only by polishing yourself through repeated difficulties can you build a self that sparkles as brightly as a gem. When you have developed such a state of being, nothing will faze you. You will be free. You will be victorious. Hardships will even become enjoyable. Daring to take on tough challenges — that in itself is immense freedom.

Freedom is relative. You may run away from hard work and effort, declaring yourself a free spirit, but you cannot run away from yourself — from your own weaknesses, personality and destiny. It is like trying to run from your own shadow. It is even more impossible to escape from the sufferings of aging, sickness and death inherent in the human condition. The more you try to avoid hardships, the more doggedly they pursue you, like so many relentless hounds chasing at your heels. That's why it's important that you turn and face your troubles head-on. It is impossible to have absolutely everything go your way all the time. In fact, if it weren't for the various obstacles life presents us with, we probably wouldn't appreciate what it is to be free.

The springtime of our youth is meant to be lived with

our faces turned toward the sun. As a season of growth, youth is a time of both great joy and great suffering. It is filled with problems and worries of all kinds. But rather than run away from them, the key is to keep seeking the sun, to keep moving in the direction of the sunlight, to challenge the pain and agony that are part of growing up.

Never give in to defeat. For a seed to sprout, it must exert tremendous effort to break out of its hard outer covering. That sprout must then valiantly push its way up through a thick layer of soil to reach the blue sky above. The hardships you experience now will all contribute to your growth. Therefore, the important thing is to keep pressing forward no matter how tough or painful the going may get.

Youth is the time to develop a spirit of persistence. And those who keep striving for improvement remain youthful no matter what their age. Conversely, those who fail to do so, even if they are young in years, will be old and weak in spirit.

Life is a battle to win ultimate and unlimited freedom. Buddhism teaches the concept of using our negative tendencies and sufferings as springboards to happiness, to forging within our lives a state of unsurpassed freedom.

C
O
N
F
I
D
E
N
C
E

BRING OUT YOUR BEST

I don't like my personality. Is it possible to change it?

Many people believe personality is determined by fate or heredity and there's nothing we can do about it. The fact is, almost everyone agonizes over some aspect of his or her personality. But you have to realize that just worrying about your problems won't change anything. When you become aware of your shortcomings, you are in a position to begin to control them and change your behavior.

People's personalities are truly diverse. There is a vast vocabulary to describe personalities and character traits. The English language is said to have as many as eighteen thousand nouns and adjectives that describe character.

No one's personality is flawless. We all, without exception, have qualities that render us less than perfect. Inevitably, you won't like aspects of your personality. But it is foolish to become obsessed by such things and succumb to feelings of self-hatred and unworthiness. You will only hinder your growth.

Being introverted doesn't make someone incapable, just as being quick-tempered doesn't make a person useless. For example, a person's shyness can be transformed into valuable qualities such as prudence and discretion, while someone's impatience might be transformed into a knack for getting things done quickly and efficiently. We should live in a way that is true to ourselves. That is the fundamental aim of Buddhism. So even though our basic personality may be difficult to change, we can bring out its positive traits.

Your personality is like a river. At a certain point, the

river's banks are pretty much fixed. In the same way, the identity of a person doesn't change much. But the quality of the water in the river can vary. It may be deep or shallow, polluted or clean, have lots of fish or none at all. While our river can't become a completely different sort of river, we can, through our hard work, purify it so that many kinds of fish will be happy to swim in it.

Our personality doesn't determine our happiness or unhappiness. Rather it is the substance of our lives and how we've lived that decide our happiness. The purpose of Buddhism and education, as well as all our efforts toward self-improvement and growth, is to enhance that substance. This is what life is all about. When Buddhists chant Nam-myoho-renge-kyo each day, one result is that they cleanse their lives of negativity and impurities, pushing everything in the direction of happiness.

A river meanders but never stops. This is the natural way of things. Similarly, if you make continual efforts, your personality will improve slowly, steadily. The key is to keep moving forward and never stop.

All rivers, irrespective of their differences, flow unceasingly and unflaggingly to the sea. If we, too, continue to make persistent efforts, we will eventually reach the great ocean of happiness for ourselves and others. We will savor boundless freedom and realize our own potential as we celebrate and encourage others' individuality.

The important thing is to do everything you possibly can. You'll be more surprised than anyone at how much you can achieve. You possess such unlimited potential!

CONFIDENCE

NATURE VS. NURTURE

Is who we are determined by our genes, our environment, or both?

I imagine it's a little of both. And, of course, many studies have been conducted on this subject. Essentially, however, we are the architects of our own lives. More important is to know that we are the architects of the *rest* of our lives.

The word *character* derives from the Greek *charakter*, meaning to engrave or make an impression upon. From a scientific standpoint, personality and physical constitution may be determined to some extent by our genes. But knowing that alone won't change anything. What matters is what we do to improve ourselves.

Buddhism stresses the importance of the present and the future. These are what matter. That is why what we do right now is so important. Always challenging ourselves from this moment onward — this is Buddhism.

Personality is also viewed a number of ways by psychologists. One view looks at personality in terms of concentric circles. At our core lies our most basic nature. Around that is the basic personality shaped during childhood by habit and custom. Surrounding that circle is the part we form to cope with various circumstances.

Though our core personality may remain unchanged, other aspects can sometimes change so much that people around us may comment that we seem like a completely different person. In any event, we have to be true to ourselves. We have to follow our path and do our best to contribute to society. Education equips us with what we need to do that.

CHANGING KARMA

What does it mean to change your karma? Isn't everything predetermined?

Buddhism, which is founded on the law of cause and effect, stresses the concept of karma. This principle explains that life at each moment is subject to the cumulative effects of causes made in the past. What we do, what we say, and what we think are all causes. And according to Buddhism, the moment we do something, say something or think something, an effect is registered in the depths of our being. Then, as our lives meet the right circumstances, the effect becomes apparent. Personality traits are strongly connected to our karma. The good news is that, unlike fate, our karma can be changed by causes we make from this moment forward. In fact, the practice of Buddhism is essentially the practice of continually changing our karma.

Whether we practice Buddhism or not, we can significantly improve our current situation by making a strong determination to make better causes from now on. We need not despair, as all our good causes will bring about, over time, a noticeable improvement in our circumstances.

CONFIDENCE

SEEING BEYOND FAULTS

How can I focus on my good points instead of my faults?

People who are critical of themselves often worry about this — it's a sign of a sincere, praiseworthy character.

It's difficult to see ourselves objectively. But, remember, no one has only faults or only merits. We all have a mixture of both. Therefore, we should strive to develop and polish our positive attributes. As we do, our shortcomings will fade until they are no longer apparent.

Perhaps you could ask someone who knows you well, a friend, parent or sibling, what strong points he or she thinks you have and can develop. I'm sure they'll name many admirable qualities. Also, if someone close to you points out your faults, rather than becoming offended or upset, it is to your benefit to listen calmly and objectively to what he or she has to say and make an effort to take it as constructive criticism. Once you take your place in society, there won't be many people who will be so honest with you.

HANDLING CRITICISM

It is hard for me to stop thinking about things that upset me — especially when I feel criticized or put down.

Sensitivity is a personality trait. In and of itself, it is neither good nor bad. But if you have that trait, you can choose to turn it into a plus.

For example, should a friend criticize you, you could turn it into a positive by thinking deeply about what has been said so you can correct a possible fault. Whatever has been said, however, is certainly not something you need to worry over. If you feel stung, take a moment to congratulate yourself on having the capacity for humility and self-reflection. People who are indifferent often lack any perspective for self-improvement.

My mentor, Josei Toda, taught me about this, showing me that the best way to avoid losing confidence or falling into needless despair over criticism is to learn to be a good listener. Instead of becoming defensive or thinking immediately that you are hopeless, choose to allow yourself to be stimulated toward further personal growth. Actively listen to what is being said in order to find the positive nugget.

That having been said, after sifting through the criticism for whatever value there might be, it is very important that you are determined not to brood over it or withdraw into your shell.

C
O
N
F
I
D
E
N
C
E

SHYNESS

I'm too shy to speak to others, and I don't like forcing myself.

If you are not talkative, how about becoming an excellent listener? You can say to others: "Please tell me about yourself. I want to hear all about you." If you try to make people think you're something that you're not, then speaking will be nothing but torture. You are fine just the way you are. Let people get to know the real you, warts and all.

Some people just ramble on mindlessly without saying anything. A person of few words is likely to speak with far more substance and depth than someone who talks just to hear his or her own voice! Someone who takes action swiftly and effectively is a great deal more trustworthy than someone who is all talk.

Of far greater importance than whether you are quiet or talkative is whether you have rich inner substance. The beautiful smile or small, unconscious gesture of a person with a rich heart, even if he or she is quiet, will speak more eloquently than any words. And often such people will speak out with authority and confidence at a crucial moment.

In Buddhism, we say the voice does the Buddha's work. Fundamentally, this refers to chanting Nam-myoho-renge-kyo. We chant to become happy ourselves. But we also chant for others' happiness. This allows us to approach them from a place of compassion. Quite naturally, then, we develop the capacity to freely, confidently say what we want to say.

SELF-CONSCIOUSNESS

I am self-conscious and easily intimidated and I often worry about what others think of me.

Timidity and shyness are signs of a gentle, sensitive nature. Perhaps you've heard of Eleanor Roosevelt, one of the most respected women in U.S. history. In her book *You Learn by Living,* she writes: "Looking back, I see how abnormally timid and shy I was as a girl. As long as I let timidity and shyness dominate me I was half paralyzed."

Through self-discipline, Mrs. Roosevelt conquered her problem. Like most shy people, she was plagued by fears about herself, so she applied herself earnestly to break those chains. By continually challenging herself, Mrs. Roosevelt gradually gained confidence. What concrete measures did she take? The same measures that will help you today.

She stopped worrying about making a good impression, stopped being obsessed over what others thought of her. Instead, she started caring about others' well-being. She also wholeheartedly pursued her interests. In doing so, she learned that people don't pay much attention to what others are doing and the amount of attention we pay ourselves is actually our greatest enemy. Realizing this, her self-consciousness lessened.

Third, she nurtured her sense of adventure and desire to experience life. She maintained a lively spirit for discovering what life had to offer.

The important thing is, take that first step. Bravely overcoming one small fear gives you the courage to take on the next one.

Make goals. Whether big or small, work toward realizing

C
O
N
F
I
D
E
N
C
E

them. Please be serious about and committed to your goals; you'll get nowhere if you treat them lightly. An earnest, dedicated spirit shines like a diamond and moves people's hearts. That is because a brilliant flame burns within.

It is pointless to be caught up in outward appearances. If we are sincere, people will understand our intentions, and our positive qualities will radiate.

It's all about taking action. If your aim is to swim across a vast ocean, it will do you no good to get cold feet before you even take the plunge. Rather, you need to make a move, keeping your sights on your goal in the distance. Hindsight can be valuable, but it is self-defeating to set yourself up for failure before even trying.

The German poet Goethe wrote: "How may one get to know oneself? Never by contemplation, only, indeed, by action. Seek to do your duty, and you will know at once how it is with you."

VIEWING OTHERS POSITIVELY

Most of my fellow students and the adults I know seem stupid and out of it.

It's much more valuable to look for the strengths in others — you gain nothing by criticizing people's imperfections. In fact, it is helpful to take a step back, for even a moment each day, and try to consider the feelings and positive qualities of others of whom you are critical. In Buddhism, we are encouraged to chant for the happiness of those who, for whatever reason, displease, anger or even hurt us. Often this is not easy. But, inevitably, we come to see the better side of most people.

For as long as we move forward and continue to grow, we can't help facing problems and inner struggles. Those of us who practice Buddhism know that we cannot change our circumstances and environment — including the people around us — without changing ourselves. If we keep challenging ourselves without giving up, we will definitely cultivate tolerance and broad-mindedness and be happier for it.

C
O
N
F
I
D
E
N
C
E

COMPASSION

8

- Concern for Others

- True Kindness

- Helping Courageously

- Showing You Care

- Touching People's Lives

- Facing Insensitivity

- Stopping Bullies

- Dealing With Violence

- Violence Toward Women

COMPASSION

CONCERN FOR OTHERS

It seems like people are so mean to one another these days. Even among my peers, I find most of them are unconcerned with the well-being of others.

How people deal with others, particularly those who are in a less fortunate position, indicates a great deal about character. *A single instance of consideration can leave an indelible impression.*

When I was around twelve, I delivered newspapers. I wanted to do whatever I could to help my family since my brothers had gone off to fight in World War II. Our family business was farming seaweed, so there were many chores, starting early in the morning. Afterward, while the town still slept, I would go on my paper route. I remember riding my bike in the bitter cold wind, my breath coming out in white puffs, my fingers frozen to the bone. I rarely saw the faces of the families on my paper route, but on the odd occasion I did, they weren't friendly. Even their dogs gave me a hard time.

But I will never forget the warmth and consideration shown to me by one young couple. One day, the young wife was bringing a charcoal stove into the hallway to cook rice. I said good morning and handed her the paper. Greeting me with a warm smile, she thanked me and commented that I was always in high spirits. Handing me a bundle of thick slices of dried sweet potatoes (a Japanese treat), she explained that they had been sent from her hometown in northern Japan the previous day. She said, "I hope you'll enjoy these" and sent her regards to my parents.

On another occasion, after I finished my evening

C
O
M
P
A
S
S
I
O
N

deliveries, the couple invited me to stay for dinner. They asked many questions about my family. I told them about my father, who had fallen seriously ill and was bedridden. The husband, to encourage me, said: "People who struggle when they're young are truly fortunate. Study hard and you will achieve great things." Though these incidents took place sixty years ago, the great kindness and concern they showed me remain etched in my heart to this day.

TRUE KINDNESS

I try to treat people fairly. Isn't that enough?

Being considerate is a matter of the heart. The word *consideration* in the Japanese language is made up of the pictographs for "person" and for "concern." Thus, to be considerate is to have concern for others, to empathize with them especially when they are struggling with sadness, pain and loneliness. These pictographs can also mean "excellent." A genuinely considerate person, one who understands another's heart, is an exceptional human being, an honors student of life. To have such concern for others is to live in the most humane way. It is a sign of outstanding character.

Being kindhearted, however, is not the same as being considerate. Being considerate means taking action on your kindhearted feelings. This is especially true when injustice occurs. In fact, we display weakness by not taking action at a crucial moment.

To be considerate means that the more individuals are suffering, the more difficult their behavior is, the more love you show them. Doing so gives you the courage to help another. Consideration also means recognizing another person's unhappiness for what it is, trying to understand and share his or her suffering. This will enable you to grow and at the same time help the other person become strong. Consideration is active; it is training ourselves in the art of encouraging others.

The important thing is not just to sympathize with or pity others but to understand what they are going through. Empathy is crucial. Sometimes having someone who understands can give others the strength to go on.

C
O
M
P
A
S
S
I
O
N

Many people treasure consideration in others and want to be considerate but, at the same time, don't want to get too involved. These people have a mistaken idea of what being considerate is; they think it means keeping a safe distance from others so as not to hurt them or be hurt. But, on the contrary, being considerate means allowing yourself to be close to others and valuing and respecting each person's dignity.

I'm reminded of a story about a warmhearted Japanese schoolteacher, deeply loved by all his students. When he was asked about the decisive turning point in his life, he spoke of an incident from his childhood. One cold winter day, a mother and her daughter, who performed in the streets for handouts, came to his house. The mother played a stringed instrument and sang while the daughter danced. A light snow was falling, and he had just come from the store with a bag of pastries. He sat eating them as he watched the performers. When the song ended, he meagerly offered the girl a half-eaten pastry.

Seeing this, his father ran to him angrily and scolded him. The father turned to the performers, bowed deeply and apologized for his son's lack of generosity. He also insisted that his son bow and apologize. After giving the mother and daughter small sacks of rice, he took his son's remaining pastries and handed them to the girl.

The father wanted to drive home to his son that all people are equal and worthy of respect. As the boy grew up, he never forgot this lesson and became known for his kindness to others.

Also, I am reminded of the founding president of our organization, Tsunesaburo Makiguchi, who became a noted school principal in Tokyo. When he was an elementary school teacher in Hokkaido, during snowstorms, he would go out to meet his students as they arrived. He would also always have hot water ready in the schoolroom to gently soak the children's frozen hands, asking them: "How's that? Does it feel better?"

Later, Mr. Makiguchi was teaching at a school where the students came from poor families. In addition to taking care of the eight members of his own family, he would, before leaving home, prepare lunches for the children who came to school without them. He would place the lunches in an inconspicuous spot where the needy children could get them without feeling embarrassed.

The human heart's capacity for compassion is very great.

C
O
M
P
A
S
S
I
O
N

HELPING COURAGEOUSLY

What if you're rejected or even ridiculed for trying to help someone? Or if offering help offends the other person?

Certainly there's no knowing how another will respond. Sometimes your sincere intentions will be completely rejected or you may be laughed at or even ridiculed. Remember, though, if this happens, turning around and getting angry at the person you're trying to help does nobody any good. Letting fear paralyze you is foolish, too.

Ultimately, what matters is your intention. Please have the courage to follow your instincts when it comes to helping people. Your life will expand only as much as you take action on behalf of others, regardless of how they may react to your kindness. Consideration equals strength, so the more considerate of others you are, the stronger you will become.

Tsunesaburo Makiguchi, the first Soka Gakkai president, hated to see people just stand by and do nothing. He believed that the good but fainthearted, in failing to fight evil, are ultimately defeated by it. Mr. Makiguchi often said:

> *Not doing good is effectively the same as doing bad. Let's say someone places a huge boulder in the middle of the road. This is malicious, as it will cause trouble for those who pass by. Then, someone comes along and sees the large obstruction, but, even knowing that it will cause serious problems, leaves it there with the attitude "Well, I didn't put it there." This may seem like an innocuous response, but, actually, not moving the boulder is causing the same inconvenience for the future passersby as putting it there in the first place.*

Most people have a spark of warmth or human kindness in their hearts. No one is born coldhearted. But if, as time passes, people bury their warmth deep in their hearts for fear of being hurt, they will become cold and hard. Similarly, those who are self-centered and think everyone is against them tend to gird themselves with the armor of callousness or conceit. Such behavior is devoid of humanity.

The Buddha always initiated dialogue with people to help them cope with their sufferings. He didn't wait for others to speak to him first, nor did it ever occur to him to worry about what they might think of him. He addressed people warmly and with ease.

SHOWING YOU CARE

What's the best way to help other people?

W hat's crucial is the sincere wish to see others become happy. And it is something we should make some effort toward each day. Mr. Makiguchi often talked about classifying goodness into acts of small, medium and great good. This applies to consideration as well: small, medium and great consideration.

For example, imagine that you have a friend who constantly needs money. Giving your friend money is an act of small good, whereas helping your friend find a job is an act of medium good.

If your friend is suffering because of a tendency to be irresponsible and lazy, however, then neither a gift of money nor a job will help. The money will be squandered, and your friend will doubtless lose the job through his or her negative habits. Great good means helping that person face and uproot the lazy nature that is the source of your friend's suffering — in other words, demonstrating and helping to teach a correct belief system.

Those who practice the self-empowering teaching of Nichiren Buddhism, which enables people to take control of their lives and refresh their determination to live victoriously each day, know that it's not enough just to work on becoming happy themselves. None of us can be fully happy if others around us are struggling. Therefore, Buddhist practitioners find that the most considerate and caring thing they can do is to share these teachings with others.

Often, attempts to do great good are misunderstood. No doubt, you, too, may meet some resentment when you try to help someone through your great consideration. But, though your efforts may not be valued now, as long as you act with the utmost sincerity, people will come to trust and rely on you. They will in time be truly grateful for the love and kindness and ultimate act of consideration you have shown them.

C
O
M
P
A
S
S
I
O
N

TOUCHING PEOPLE'S LIVES

I would like to be the kind of person who can really touch people's lives in some way.

A person's nobility is manifested in compassion for others. Kindness and consideration for others resonate with both the Buddhist concept of compassion and the core Christian concept of love. When viewed from a larger perspective, we exist here thanks to the warmth, kindness and support not only of the people around us but of everything on this Earth and in the entire universe.

All living things — flowers, birds, the sun, the soil — support one another in a beautiful symphony of life. Since the birth of this planet more than four billion years ago, life form after life form has been conceived and nourished. Human life is a part of that chain. If at any point a link were missing from this chain, none of us would be alive today. We are all proof that the chain hasn't been broken.

Life produces new life — surely this is consideration in its most basic form. Delving deeper into this idea, I think we can say that the Earth itself is a giant living organism filled with consideration. The activity of the entire universe is essentially a function of compassion.

Truly commendable people have the spirit to improve and grow, and continually striving to develop ourselves above all else is true consideration for others.

FACING INSENSITIVITY

I always get picked on because I'm disabled.

Those who laugh and make fun of you are cruel and wrong-minded. They create a terrible burden of negative karma for themselves by ignoring your right to be treated as a human being and respected. But letting their taunts get to you is a defeat for you as a human being. Your strength, however, is a victory.

So, essentially, you have to become stronger. Yours, too, is part of the human-rights struggle. Having your rights recognized by others is not just having people behave sympathetically. Be proud of yourself as an individual, regardless of your disability. Be proud of your mission in life. To be considerate, we need to be strong. We also need to be strong to defend human rights, not just ours but those of others.

STOPPING BULLIES

I see so much discrimination and bullying in my immediate surroundings.

Bullying is war in miniature. Pettiness, arrogance, jealousy and self-centeredness — all those base and destructive emotions violate human rights. On a larger scale, they manifest as war and crime.

Whatever the reason, bullying is wrong. Maybe those who bully others have their excuses — maybe they want to take out their pain on others. But whatever the reason or motive, bullying and discrimination are impossible to justify.

Ultimately, bullying is a crime against humanity. Part of the fight for human rights is standing up to those doing destructive, painful things to others. Another part of that fight is protecting good people.

When you can't get the bullies to stop picking on others through your own efforts, talk to someone whom you trust. Think very hard of some way to improve the situation.

Whatever happens, please don't put yourself down if you can't solve the problem. Even if you find you cannot do or say anything right now, it's important to recognize that those who are picking on you or someone else are wrong.

If you leap into the fray and only get beaten up yourself, it won't solve anything. Rather than deciding you're useless, concentrate on developing yourself so that you can effect a positive change in the future.

DEALING WITH VIOLENCE

Many young people are becoming violent. Some are even proud of it. Is there anything I can do?

I understand that following the Colorado tragedy at Columbine High School, in which thirteen students were shot to death, President Clinton said, "We must reach out to our children and teach them to express their anger and to resolve their conflicts with words, not weapons." I fully agree. Nothing makes my heart ache more than the fact that young people, who possess infinite potential for the future, destroy their own lives and those of others.

When I was young, I lost my eldest brother to World War II. He was a kindhearted person who disagreed vehemently with Japan's course of action. Agonizing over Japan's invasion of China, he said: "The Japanese army is heartless. I feel terribly sorry for the Chinese people."

I'll never forget the image of my mother from behind, her tiny back shuddering in sorrow at the news of her eldest son's death in the war. Even then, I deeply felt we should abolish war and violence from this earth, no matter what.

While of course it is vital to control the external elements of violence by abolishing weapons, developing more adequate laws and establishing peace agreements among nations, ultimately what's needed is to understand that violence arises from an innate human condition. Buddhism terms this condition *animality*, a state where one is swayed by instinctive desires and has no sense of reason or morality. Even if we may have wiped out all the weapons from this planet, violence will never perish unless we successfully control the animality within us. For this very reason, we

COMPASSION

need to change the human condition from within.

I have often called for something like a humanitarian competition, where all religions that teach tolerance and concern compete to see how many caring individuals they can each foster. In any case, education based on the dignity of each individual is the key.

Violence is an absolute evil. No matter how correct what you say is, if you resort to violence to prove it, you are a loser. Even if you appear to triumph as a result of violent action, you will end up losing.

Buddhism stresses the interconnectedness of all life. It is only the limited capacity of our senses that causes us to place so much stock in the separation between "them" and "us." Because of this interconnectedness, by using violence, you not only injure or destroy the other person but also yourself. Those who use violence and devalue others' lives actually devalue themselves and ruin their own lives.

It's important to understand that the essence of violence is cowardice. Because a person is cowardly, he or she turns to violence. This individual lacks the courage to have dialogue. Mahatma Gandhi said eloquently that "Nonviolence is not a cover for cowardice, but it is the supreme virtue of the brave.... Cowardice is wholly inconsistent with nonviolence.... Nonviolence presupposes the ability to strike."

The ability to dialogue is proof of one's intellect. Of course, the top leaders of the nation are mainly responsible for the plight of modern society where violence is common. Adults in the fields of politics, education and the media share the blame. Just criticizing them, however, will not change a thing. There is no other way than for you to stand up individually, believing that your efforts can contribute to building a different society from now on. You can start by enlarging the nonviolent circle in your immediate environment.

Within the Soka Gakkai International, American youth have been carrying out activities to call an end to violence. They are putting the following three pledges into action.

1. I will value my own life.
2. I will respect all life.
3. I will inspire hope in others.

As we each become able to cherish our own lives, we will naturally be able to value others' lives as well.

The important thing is that you do something. Starting is the first step. Zero is zero even if multiplied by other numbers. But as the saying in the Orient goes, "One is the mother of tens of thousands."

C
O
M
P
A
S
S
I
O
N

VIOLENCE TOWARD WOMEN

These days, there seems to be an increase in physical and sexual violence toward women. What can be done?

Nothing is so vulgar as violence toward women. Violence must not be tolerated. All men should remember this, and they should look upon their female contemporaries as sisters whose lives are to be cherished. Shame on men if they are not gentle.

At the same time, it is crucial for women to protect themselves with wisdom and prudence. Many groups exist to help women. When you realize how precious your life is, you'll do everything possible to protect it. It is also very important to heed the advice of parents and friends you can trust.

Victims of violence are often deeply hurt spiritually as well as physically. They lose trust in their humanity and often feel tarnished as if their lives have been destroyed. If you were a victim of violence, please remember that, no matter what, your value as an individual will never change. Brace yourself firmly. Say to yourself, "I am not a person who will allow such an incident to destroy my life." No one can destroy your life on the deepest level. No matter how much you may have been hurt, you can retain your fundamental dignity — no one can take that from you without your consent.

Buddhism teaches the principle that the pure white lotus grows out of a muddy pond. Likewise, a supreme state of life can grow while living amidst the most painful reality.

No matter how down you may feel, there is someone somewhere suffering in a similar manner, and you in particular can help that person because of your common understanding. And there is the true affection in others' hearts that especially you can discover. You may not feel much like relating your troubles to others, but to have even one person you can consult with about your experiences will make all the difference in your outlook. You should not suffer all by yourself. There is incredible potential inherent within your life. If you should give up on yourself, it would be all the more terrible, because it would amplify the damage already done. Never let your suffering cause you to desert your true self.

It may seem strange, but those who have suffered the most or who have been saddened the most can become the happiest. With the tears you shed you can cleanse your life and make it shine. Forging ahead is the essence of living and the Buddhist spirit.

COMPASSION

THE BIGGER PICTURE 9

- Understanding Equality

- Courage Is the Key

- Human Rights

- World Citizenship

- Getting Started

- Friendship and Peace

- Environmental Concerns

- Practicing Environmental Protection

- Role of the Individual

UNDERSTANDING EQUALITY

The world is filled with hatred. What can one person do?

U nless we build a society that regards human beings not
as means to a goal but as the goal itself, we will remain
forever deadlocked in inequality, unhappiness and violence
— what Buddhism terms a world of animality, where the
strong prey upon the weak. We will simply repeat the same
patterns.

It is vital that we teach the citizens of all nations to see
themselves and others first and foremost as human beings.
We have to raise people's awareness of human rights
through education. Our schools must teach human rights,
our religions must teach human rights and our governments
must respect human rights.

A child's heart does not discriminate. If they aren't
taught discrimination by others, children of all races play
happily together. And children are not the least bit interested in how well-off the families of their playmates are or
what kind of work their parents do. They assume that all
human beings are equal.

In the depths of our lives, we each possess a precious
jeweled sword that is uniquely our own. This mighty spiritual sword pierces through negative forces and defends
justice. As long as we realize that we possess this inner
sword and continuously polish it for the sake of good, we
will never be defeated. We will win without fail.

This jeweled sword is our heart, our determination. If
it is not polished, it will grow dull and weak; and if it
remains sheathed, it is useless in battling obstacles. It is
not a cruel and evil sword that harms others but a spiritual

sword committed to good and benefiting others and as such is an infinitely precious treasure. Those who neither unsheathe nor polish their inner sword of justice lead fearful and timid lives. This magnificent sword is your character. Thus, to polish the sword within means to study, develop friendships and construct a solid self. To polish this inner sword is the purpose of daily Buddhist practice.

I met with Nelson Mandela, former president of South Africa, on two occasions. President Mandela endured twenty-seven and a half years — nearly ten thousand days — in prison for his anti-apartheid activities. He is an indomitable champion of human rights who brought an end to the inhuman policy of racial segregation in his country.

South Africa maintained an unparalleled state of harsh discrimination against the majority of its citizens. Under apartheid, it was a crime for black South Africans to ride a "Whites Only" bus, to use a "Whites Only" drinking fountain, to walk on a "Whites Only" beach, to be on the streets past 11:00 p.m., to travel, to be unemployed and to live in certain places. In short, black South Africans were not treated as human beings.

Filled with outrage at the unforgivable discrimination he saw all around him, Mr. Mandela became the leader of the anti-apartheid movement. Such passion for justice was the jeweled sword he wielded. He studied, worked and took a resolute stand against the government, determined to completely reform this inhumane society. He never yielded, even under the hellish conditions he suffered in prison, and he succeeded in defeating a tradition of discrimination in South Africa that had lasted almost 350 years.

Those who have suffered persecution for the sake of justice are truly noble. Mr. Mandela, who was once mocked and humiliated, is now respected all over the world.

COURAGE IS THE KEY

What is the essential ingredient in the struggle for human rights?

Only when people have the courage to stand up for justice, even if they are the only one, can they lead the world in the direction of peace and good. When such courageous individuals join forces and unite in strong solidarity, they can change society. But it all starts with you. Everything follows from your own courage.

In her book *Dear Mrs. Parks: A Dialogue with Today's Youth*, Rosa Parks, the mother of the civil rights movement in the United States, writes:

> *I had no idea that history was being made. I was just tired of giving in. Somehow, I felt that what I did was right by standing up to that bus driver. I did not think about the consequences. I knew that I could have been lynched, manhandled, or beaten when the police came. I chose not to move, because I was right.*

Mrs. Parks found the courage to speak out because she believed she was right. Courage always springs from what is right, from justice. It comes from the wish to do what's right, to build a just society, and to be a good human being.

If we are to do good, not only for ourselves but for humanity and the world as well, we need courage. Courage is the power that makes such actions possible — actions that may not call attention to the actors but really shine with the brilliance of good.

Putting an end to schoolyard bullying is an act of

courage. So are enduring hardships and surviving tough circumstances. And so is trying to live an honest, decent life day after day. In contrast, people who are lazy or who don't care or who have fallen into bad ways have not had the courage to challenge daily life. In our families and among our friends, if we clearly state our opinions things will move in a positive direction. Our willingness to proceed in that direction and help others to do so as well is a very admirable form of courage.

No matter what anyone else may say, always do what you believe is right. If you have the courage to do that, it's like having a magical weapon of unlimited powers. In Buddhism, we call such a person a bodhisattva, one dedicated to relieving the suffering of others.

THE BIGGER PICTURE

HUMAN RIGHTS

Why do so many governments and our own people, too, deny human rights?

Governments will only change when the people themselves, one by one, decide to honor the rights of everyone around them. Those unable to see all people as human beings the same as themselves are spiritually impoverished. They have no sound philosophy of life. They do not ponder life's more profound questions. They care only for their petty concerns. Our society is filled with people consumed by greed, who exploit the weak while fawning on the strong, thinking power will bring them fulfillment. These negative tendencies are what make our society discriminate against and ignore human rights.

Humans also tend to reject and attack anything the least bit different. We are all human beings. That is what matters.

Everyone has a right to flower, to reveal his or her full potential as a human being, to fulfill his or her mission in this world. You have this right, and so does everyone else. This is the meaning of human rights. To scorn, violate and abuse people's human rights destroys the natural order of things. Prizing human rights and respecting others are among our most important tasks.

WORLD CITIZENSHIP

I've heard the term "citizen of the world." What does it mean to be one?

Many people think the term *world citizen* means a person fluent in a foreign language! But there is more involved. A world citizen is one who can easily make friends with people from other countries, one who doesn't assume that the values of his or her nation apply everywhere else in the world, and one who can adopt a global perspective, looking beyond the boundaries of ethnicity.

It also includes all those working for world peace, praying earnestly for the happiness of all humanity and selflessly working for the sake of others. People who feel a sense of responsibility toward the world's future and who understand those earnestly taking action can call themselves world citizens as well. So, essentially, to become a world citizen, it is necessary to develop your character and sense of humanity, your willingness to work for the welfare of people and society.

There is a famous story about Chiune Sugihara, who — much like Oskar Schindler of *Schindler's List* fame — helped Jewish refugees escape the Holocaust during World War II. In 1940, Sugihara was acting consul at the Japanese consulate in Lithuania. A wave of Jewish refugees from Poland, where Jews were being massacred, came to Sugihara to apply for transit visas to pass through Japan to a third country. Three times Sugihara asked the Japanese Ministry of Foreign Affairs to give him the green light to issue the visas, but each time the ministry refused. He was deeply troubled but finally came to a decision: "I couldn't abandon those who came to me for help. If I did, I would be turning my

THE BIGGER PICTURE

back on God." So he ignored the orders and issued the visas, saving nearly six thousand lives.

After the war, Sugihara was forced to resign from the ministry for disobeying orders. In 1991, the ministry posthumously restored his good name. His widow, Sachiko, said in a newspaper interview: "The lives of all people are precious, irrespective of race. My husband believed it was not right for a human being to refuse to help those in need, especially when in a position to do something."

The true world citizen can share, as a fellow human being, the sufferings and sadness as well as the happiness and joy of others regardless of their nationality or ethnic background. This person can unite with others to promote common human interests.

Keeping one's word is important as a world citizen. Politicians, even in my own country, have a reputation for making promises when they visit other nations, then forgetting them as soon as they set foot on home soil. That's certainly no way to earn others' trust.

Friendship is the key. To never betray one's friendship, to nurture and develop strong, amicable ties — these are the qualities required of a world citizen.

Perhaps some among you think, "What's being a world citizen got to do with me?" But, like it or not, in this century when you take your place in society, the world is going to become even more integrated.

The Egyptian president, Hosni Mubarak, shared with me the following observation he once heard from another dignitary: No country today can even produce a box of matches by itself. The matchstick comes from one nation, the sulfur from another, the box from another and the glue from yet another. Many countries must cooperate to produce even a single box of matches.

The globalization of goods and production is taking place incredibly swiftly, as is the globalization of information, especially with the growth of the Internet. For these reasons, the globalization of heart-to-heart, grass-roots exchange is absolutely critical in guiding these rapid changes in the direction of peace.

THE BIGGER PICTURE

GETTING STARTED

What can I do to make a difference in terms of human rights?

Y ou can start by reading good literature. You will find many human rights issues explored in the pages of such works.

Even more important, you can learn to recognize the positive qualities of others. One of the first steps in achieving human rights is appreciating and embracing individuality in others.

It's also important to develop a solid perspective about humanity, realizing that though others may be different from you, we are all members of the same human family. According to one scientist, the ability to differentiate operates in a very shallow level of the brain, while the ability to find commonalities involves highly sophisticated information-processing in a much deeper level.

Those who can get along with all kinds of people, seeing them as equals, as fellow human beings, manifest the true excellence of their character. They are people of genuine culture and education.

The richer our hearts, our humanity, the more we can recognize and value the humanity of others. Those who bully and belittle others only diminish their humanity.

Human rights are the sun illuminating the world. So, too, are love of humanity, kindness and consideration. All these light our world. Their light brings cherry, plum and peach into glorious bloom in society, enabling everyone to reveal their unique potential.

Your mission is to make the sun of human rights rise

over the twenty-first century. To do that, first make the courageous sun of love for humanity rise in your own heart. Francis William Bourdillon expressed this beautifully in his poem "Light."

> *The night has a thousand eyes,*
> *And the day but one;*
> *Yet the light of the bright world dies*
> *With the dying sun.*
> *The mind has a thousand eyes,*
> *And the heart but one;*
> *Yet the light of a whole life dies*
> *When love is done.*

THE BIGGER PICTURE

FRIENDSHIP AND PEACE

What role does friendship play in creating a peaceful world?

Friendship is one of the main foundations of what it means to be human. It's an important driving force for world peace and the betterment of society. It is the first step toward realizing a society where people can live together in harmony. By expanding our circle of friendship, we can create the foundation for a peaceful society.

In an ideal world, all people would be friends. But we know that this is unfortunately not the case in the world today. That's why it is so important that we actively forge friendships with as many people as we can. We must face the challenges of reality and make what changes we can, small as they may be. The accumulation of such efforts will gradually lead to lasting world peace.

When expounding his teachings, Shakyamuni Buddha always addressed "all living beings." I think the phrase "all living beings" itself incorporates this universal spirit of friendship — the spirit that treats every person and every living thing as equally precious and worthy of respect and seeks to bring happiness to all.

I am very proud to have many friends of outstanding character and ability throughout the world. And I have these friends because I have always valued each encounter and treasured each person. Even the most ambitious undertakings actually come down to one-on-one relationships accumulating over the years. It's always one-on-one — always.

Many years of experience have led me to conclude that nothing is nobler or stronger than heart-to-heart bonds among people who share their hopes and dreams and are committed to working for society. Such people have deep-rooted conviction and a solid philosophy. They strive to lead a worthwhile existence and contribute something of value to their respective societies. Unity and cooperation among people of such altruistic aspiration are the highest ideals of friendship. If such lofty friendship ceases to exist, the world will be plunged into eternal darkness.

Our individual circle of friendship is part of the global circle of friendship; it is one and the same. A drop of rain from the sky, a drop of water from the river, or a drop of water from the ocean are all just that — a drop of water — until they accumulate. The friends we make in our own small circle contribute to the spread of friendship around the world. Making one true friend is a step toward creating world peace.

THE BIGGER PICTURE

ENVIRONMENTAL CONCERNS

I'm concerned about the environment. Isn't there something really wrong with the path we humans are taking?

Yes. The destruction of nature is the destruction of humanity. Nature is our home. All life on this planet, including, of course, human life, was born from the natural environment. We don't owe our existence to machines or science. Life on this planet was not artificially created. We are the products of nature.

There are many theories about the origins of humanity. Some say that the first humans appeared in Africa; others say that human beings appeared in various locations around the world at about the same time. Whatever may be true, it is indisputable that the human species was born of nature.

Because of that, the further we alienate ourselves from nature, the more unbalanced we become. Our future as a species is grim unless we recognize this.

Our problem is not new. The eighteenth-century French philosopher and social reformer Jean-Jacques Rousseau, author of *The Social Contract*, called for a return to nature. Civilization, even in his time, had become too mechanical, too reliant on science, too concentrated on profit, distorting human life into ugliness. Rousseau protested this unfortunate development.

Indeed, we all want to be healthy. For that reason, we want to breathe clean air, to see beautiful flowers and greenery. We turn to nature for this, just as a sunflower turns to the sun. We must recognize that any action negating this inclination is a terrible mistake. All the money in the world won't buy the blue sky. The sun and the breeze belong to everyone.

No one is denying that science has improved our lives. But we need to match the progress of science with progress in our commitment to preserve and protect our environment. We need a balance.

For instance, we must remember the forests. Where does the oxygen that we breathe, that keeps us alive, come from? From forests, from sea plants. It has taken plants billions of years to create this oxygen.

What about water? Most of the water we use comes from river systems. Whether it rains or shines, water flows through rivers. Why? The trees and the soil around them absorb the water, storing it underground, from where it seeps constantly, bit by bit, into the rivers. If there were no forests and the mountains were hard as asphalt, all the rain that fell in a day would run immediately into the rivers and flow out to sea, just like a bathtub emptying when you pull the plug.

Soil is another gift of the forest. Small animals and microbes help transform the dead roots and leaves of trees into rich soil. Without that soil, we could not grow grains or vegetables. We would have no food, and humanity would perish.

Many other products come from forests. Without them, we would have no rubber bands, no paper, no wooden desks or furniture — no homes. All of these, too, are the forest's gifts.

Forests produce the air we breathe, the water we drink, the soil in which we grow food — indeed, every aspect of our lives is made possible by trees.

And I think we rarely make the connection that unless we take care of the forests, we won't be able to catch fish in the sea. Without forests all the rain would flow away down the rivers to the sea. That rain would also carry large

THE BIGGER PICTURE

amounts of silt with it. The silt would cloud the sea waters, block the penetration of light, and lower the sea's temperature, making it too cold for many fish.

The forests also produce nutrients that eventually make their way to the sea and become food for marine life. The forests protect the life of the sea.

Life is a chain. All things are related. When any link is disturbed, the other links will be affected. We should think of the environment as our mother — Mother Soil, Mother Sea, Mother Earth. There is no crime worse than harming one's mother.

ENVIRONMENTAL CONCERNS

Don't environmental problems concern everyone?

Yes. Buddhism explains life in a system of ten stages or states of being — the states of Hell, Hunger, Animality, Anger, Humanity, Rapture, Learning, Realization, Bodhisattva and Buddhahood. The state of Humanity is right in the middle, with nobler states of life above and uglier states below. Those states below are unnatural states of being, states that oppose nature. The five stages above Humanity all value nature and strive to create a paradise where its beauty flourishes in abundance.

The question is whether we allow ourselves to be dragged down to the lower states or advance to the higher states. Only intelligence, culture and religious faith can lead us out of the animality that thoughtlessly consumes nature, leaving a barren wasteland. According to the Buddhist principle of the oneness of life and its environment, a barren, destructive mind produces a barren, devastated natural environment. The desertification of our planet is linked to the desertification of the human spirit.

War is the most extreme example of this destructive impulse. War destroys both nature and the human spirit. The twentieth century was a century of war. We must make this century a century of life. The twenty-first century must be one in which we make life the top priority in all spheres of human activity — in commerce, in government, in science.

We are dependent on the Earth, not the other way around. In our arrogance, we have flagrantly overlooked this. The Soviet cosmonaut Yuri Gagarin, the first person to

THE BIGGER PICTURE

see the Earth from space, declared it a blue planet. This is a great testimony. The blue of the oceans, the white of the clouds — they are proof that Earth is the water planet, a planet sparkling with life. That's why I think it's important to have a philosophy that recognizes everything in the universe as living and sacred.

The essential teaching of Buddhism is that the life of the Buddha resides in every plant and tree, even in the smallest dust mote. It's a philosophy founded on a profound reverence for life.

PRACTICING ENVIRONMENTAL PROTECTION

How do we cope with seemingly small problems, like littering?

To throw trash or aluminum cans by the roadside is the selfish behavior of someone living in a state that Buddhism terms the world of Animality. Such actions demonstrate an egoism that cares nothing for others. It is an unnatural way to live. A person who loves nature is simply unable to litter. Tossing one's trash away carelessly is to toss away one's humanity.

By the same token, one who loves nature can cherish other human beings, value peace and possess a richness of character unfettered by selfish calculations of personal gain and loss. Those who live in a calculating way will end up calculating their own worth in the same manner. Such a life is limited in the extreme.

People might think there is no reward in picking up trash others have strewn about. But it's important to do this out of love for nature — without thinking about what one may or may not gain.

Only through such selfless actions can we live the best way as human beings. Because technology has advanced to the extent it has, it is more important than ever for each person to develop an awareness of environmental protection. Any apparent material improvements are illusory unless we enhance the fundamental quality of our lives.

THE BIGGER PICTURE

ROLE OF THE INDIVIDUAL

Can I as an individual make much of a difference?

Absolutely. Each individual effort is vital, and yet it is a lot easier to talk about environmental protection than to practice it. There are obstacles sometimes — and sometimes practicing it can even be life-threatening.

I wonder if you've heard of the American marine biologist Rachel Carson. She wrote a ground-breaking book called *Silent Spring*, published in 1962, which attacked the problem of pollution.

At that time, very powerful insecticides such as DDT were being used all across the United States. They seemed to be effective at first, but gradually people were beginning to sicken and show signs of being poisoned from the chemicals. Beneficial insects, fish and birds were disappearing from the landscape. With no birds to sing, Ms. Carson wrote, a silent spring awaited us.

Her book announced these facts to the public and urged that dangerous pesticides be banned. Immediately after her book was published, she was vehemently attacked.

She was attacked by the giant corporations that made huge fortunes from manufacturing pesticides — and by officials and politicians who were in the pockets of those companies — because what she said was true. Such attacks happen all the time, whenever someone tells an unpleasant truth. We must learn to see through the charades of those in power.

All those linked to the pesticide industry, even agricultural magazines, joined in a campaign to discredit her. One wrote, "Her book is more poisonous than the pesticides she condemns." State research organizations joined the campaign — research organizations that, needless to say, received large amounts of funding from the chemical companies.

It was a major campaign to silence *Silent Spring*. Even the American Medical Association stated that the effects of pesticides posed no threat to human beings when used according to the instructions by the manufacturers.

But Rachel Carson would not give up. And she went even further, declaring that pesticides were only part of the story of the poisons that were threatening our world. Eventually, she won the support of the people, and environmentalism began to spread across the United States and throughout the world. That torch of faith kept burning after she died in 1964 and has grown to dramatically transform public awareness.

Carson left these words in *The Sense of Wonder* for the younger generation: "Those who dwell, as scientists or laymen, among the beauties and mysteries of the earth are never alone or weary of life."

A Kenyan saying goes that we should treat the Earth well; it is not a gift from our parents but a loan from our children. But the adults of our day are leaving a dismal inheritance to today's young people and the children you will have. With their philosophy that making money is the most important goal of all, they are selling off your legacy — the health, culture, environment and even life that nature has protected and nurtured for so many eons.

It is your legacy, so you must act. You who have not yet forgotten the beauty and wonder of the Earth, speak out! Your struggle to protect the twenty-first century, your century, the century of life, has already begun.

One popular slogan goes, "Be kind to our planet," but in

THE BIGGER PICTURE

reality, the planet has been kind to us. Behind each of us stands not just four billion years of kindness from the Earth but the compassion of the entire universe since time without beginning. Therefore, it's important not to slander or devalue our lives. Life is the most precious of all treasures. Each of you has been given this invaluable gift and each of you is irreplaceable. Those bearers of life — the universe, the Earth and mothers — cherish their children. The most important thing for the twenty-first century is that we expand throughout society that absolute, fundamental consideration, that profound compassion toward life.

If we do so, war and the suppression of human rights will disappear. So will the destruction of the environment.

AFTERWORD

Young people are the key to the future. Yes, that's easy enough to say. But I know that many of you wonder if you can do anything really worthwhile, anything of lasting value, when the world is in such turmoil. Because you are you, though, I know you can. And you will.

Those of you who live in the United States have a unique opportunity. America offers you freedom on a grand scale, but at the same time it has its dark clouds. With all its good points and its bad points, in a way it reflects the state of our present world as a whole. So the problems you who live in America face are in that sense the problems of all people everywhere. And your success is the hope not only of America but of the entire world.

The problems you confront in your young years can hardly be solved in a day. But no matter how hopeless they seem, if you face up to them with courage, I am confident you can overcome them in time.

Keep on learning, keep on trying, keep on till you have turned defeat into final victory — that is the true way of youth.

— Daisaku Ikeda

INDEX

ABOUT THE AUTHOR

DAISAKU IKEDA is president of the Soka Gakkai International (SGI), one of the fastest growing and most dynamic Buddhist renewal movements in the world today. With twelve million members in nearly 200 countries, the SGI promotes education, international cultural exchange and the establishment of world peace. The SGI philosophy is based on the teachings of Nichiren, a thirteenth-century Japanese Buddhist teacher and reformer who, based on the Lotus Sutra, taught the sanctity of human life above all else.

As the inspirational leader for millions, Daisaku Ikeda has paid particular attention to the development of youth throughout his more than fifty years of practicing Nichiren Buddhism and forty years of worldwide leadership of the Soka Gakkai. At age nineteen, he took faith in the teachings of Nichiren and went on to succeed his mentor, Josei Toda, as the Soka Gakkai president in 1960.

A peace activist, Mr. Ikeda has traveled to more than fifty countries meeting and holding dialogues with people, including political and intellectual leaders, applying his strong belief that international understanding and the realization of peace begins with people-to-people contacts. Among the hundreds of honors and commendations given him around the world, he received the United Nations Peace Award in 1983.

Mr. Ikeda is the founder of numerous cultural and educational institutes throughout the world, including the Soka Schools system in Japan, Malaysia, Singapore and Hong Kong, as well as Soka University, whose newest branch will open in Aliso Viejo, California, in 2001.

ACKNOWLEDGMENTS

The editors would like to thank the following individuals who contributed greatly to the making of *The Way of Youth*: Carol Southern, Carolyn Porter, Alan Gadney, Sharon Gayle, Pat Loeb, Steven Sater, Julie Remke, Manoj Varghese, Jeffrey Martin and Stacey Applebaum.

MORE ON NICHIREN BUDDHISM
and its application to daily life

The following titles can be purchased from your local or
on-line bookseller, or go to the Middleway Press
Web site (www.middlewaypress.org).

Unlocking the Mysteries of Birth & Death . . . and Everything In Between
BY DAISAKU IKEDA   ISBN 0-9723267-0-7; $15.00

This introduction to Nichiren Buddhism explores the philosophical
intricacies of life and reveals the wonder inherent in the phases of
birth, aging, and death.

Core concepts of Nichiren Buddhism, such as the Ten Worlds and
the nine consciousnesses, illustrate the profundity of human existence.
This book provides Buddhists with the tools they need to fully
appreciate the connectedness of all beings and to revolutionize their
spiritual lives based on this insight. Ultimately, this is both a work of
popular philosophy and a book of compelling, compassionate inspiration for Buddhist and non-Buddhists alike that fosters a greater
understanding of Nichiren Buddhism.

The Buddha In Your Mirror: Practical Buddhism and the Search for Self
BY WOODY HOCHSWENDER, GREG MARTIN AND TED MORINO
Paperback: ISBN 0-9674697-8-3; $14.00
Hardcover: ISBN 0-9674697-1-6; $23.95

A bestselling Buddhist primer that reveals the most modern, effective and
practical way to achieve what is called enlightenment or Buddhahood.
Based on the centuries-old teaching of the Japanese Buddhist master
Nichiren, this method has been called the "direct path" to enlightenment.

"Like the Buddha, this book offers practical guidelines to overcome
difficulties in everyday life and to be helpful to others. Readers will
find these pages are like a helpful and supportive friend. I enthusi-
astically recommend it."

—DR. DAVID CHAPPELL, editor of
Buddhist Peacework: Creating Cultures of Peace

Soka Education: A Buddhist Vision for Teachers, Students and Parents
BY DAISAKU IKEDA   ISBN 0-9674697-4-0; $23.95

From the Japanese word meaning "to create value," this book presents a fresh spiritual perspective to question the ultimate purpose of education. Mixing American pragmatism with Buddhist philosophy, the goal of Soka education is the lifelong happiness of the learner.

"[Teachers] will be attracted to Soka and Ikeda's plea that educators bring heart and soul back to education."

—*TEACHER MAGAZINE*

"Ikeda's practical perscription places students' needs first, empowers teachers, and serves as a framework for global citizenship."

—GEORGE DAVID MILLER, professor, Lewis University

Choose Hope: Your Role in Waging Peace in the Nuclear Age
BY DAVID KRIEGER AND DAISAKU IKEDA
ISBN 0-9674697-6-7; $23.95

"In this nuclear age, when the future of humankind is imperiled by irrational strategies, it is imperative to restore our sanity to our policies and hope to our destiny. Only a rational analysis of our problems can lead to their solution. This book is an example par excellence of a rational approach."

—JOSEPH ROTBLAT, Nobel Peace Prize laureate